BIBLICAL BOOKS OF WISDOM

A STUDY OF PROVERBS, JOB, ECCLESIASTES, AND OTHER WISDOM LITERATURE IN THE BIBLE

JAMES M. EFIRD

D1118451

Wipf and Stock Publishers
150 West Broadway • Eugene OR 97401
2001

Biblical Books of Wisdom

By Efird, James M.
Copyright©1983 by Efird, James M.
ISBN: 1-57910-634-X

Reprinted by *Wipf and Stock Publishers*
150 West Broadway • Eugene OR 97401

Previously published by Judson Press, 1983.

In Honor and Memory of

Jameson Jones
Dean, Duke University Divinity School
February 1981—July 1982

With Deep Appreciation and Admiration

Preface

Many lay persons are puzzled when they attempt to understand the biblical books, which have come from a time and culture long since past. Their confusion is intensified, at least in part, by a prevailing concept that the biblical materials are all "of one piece," or in other words, that they are all the same kind of literature and should all be interpreted in identical ways. Too often the approach used to interpret the Bible consists in taking every phrase and every sentence as if that small portion of the text contained theological dogma in and of itself, and taking each saying as if it were to be understood in a literal manner. In such an approach, phrases and short sentences from the Scriptures are cited to support pet theories and ideas when these phrases and sentences do not carry the meaning imposed upon them. It is the task, therefore, of each person to make every effort to understand *properly* the teachings of the various biblical materials. One of the best ways to do this is to study these books from the standpoint of their literary types.

The good people at Judson Press have allowed me to write for them several books emphasizing this approach. The book on apocalyptic literature, *Daniel and Revelation: A Study of Two Extraordinary Visions,* and the more recent book on the prophetic writings, *The Old Testament Prophets Then and Now,* have been well received. We are very grateful for this positive reception. Now we turn to another literary movement that is prominently reflected in biblical materials, namely, the wisdom movement. The ideas and literary styles associated with this movement are quite conspicuous in the writings of the Old and New Testaments. Some of these writings have never really been properly understood by most lay persons, primarily because many people have not been aware that anything like a wisdom movement ever existed, much less was a significant part of the biblical tradition.

This book is written for the primary purpose of explaining to the uninitiated student what a "wisdom movement" was, how that movement developed and presented its teachings, and how the various biblical teachings that fall under the category of "wisdom" can be better understood and interpreted.

The student is urged to read each chapter in this book and then study the corresponding biblical text. Space does not allow for the quotation here of the full biblical text, but much will be lost if that text is not studied. It is hoped that this guide can be used both for private study and for group study. There are no formal questions at the conclusion of each unit because many issues and questions are already raised in the explication of the biblical materials. Since some of these issues are directly related to human existence, there can be some provocative discussion based upon the examination of these biblical materials.

I would like to express my deep gratitude to Mr. Harold L. Twiss, General Manager of Judson Press, for his continuing support and encouragement in this project and to the fine staff of Judson Press for its assistance in bringing this project to completion. My deepest appreciation, now as always, must go to my wife, Vivian, who has typed the manuscript twice and without whose encouragement this project could not have been completed.

Finally, a word is in order concerning the one to whom this book is dedicated, Dr. Jameson Jones, the Dean of the Duke University Divinity School from February 1981 until his untimely death on July 18, 1982. Dean Jones was a rare combination of academic accomplishment and spiritual sensitivity. He was a brilliant administrator, a dedicated churchman, and a devoted husband and father. It was with great dismay that we learned of the sudden passing of this genuinely good and competent man. His death has taken from us a great ecclesiastical leader, but his dreams and aspirations for the church are still part of our dream. I hope that in some way this book will reflect a small part of my genuine respect and admiration for him.

James M. Efird
Durham, North Carolina
October 1982

Contents

 ONE

Introduction

The world in which human beings live is large and frightening. In fact, if one thinks about just how small and insignificant and at the mercy of the forces of the universe human beings are, initial feelings of insecurity and fright become feelings of utter helplessness and sheer terror. Because of the relative smallness of the human creature when compared with a huge and hostile world, some method had to evolve to enable human beings to learn more about the world and thereby to deal with that world in order to make human existence less terrifying. Such knowledge could even enable people to be happy, to structure their lives, and to find some semblance of purpose and meaning in the world.

Wisdom Teaching and Method

Every civilized group, therefore, has developed in the course of its history an investigation into the mysteries of how the world operates and how people can best cope with that world. These attempts at understanding the world and its workings have taken numerous forms and utilized various methods of investigation in different groups and cultures. Some scholars have labeled this phenomenon a search for "wisdom," and they have called the subsequent investigations and methods employed by humans to gain more insight into how to cope with the world a "wisdom movement." Every society, therefore, has a wisdom movement whether it calls the phenomenon by that title or is even aware that such a set of ideas exists within the structure of the community.

One can find such ideas reflected in the biblical book of Proverbs.

> My son, keep sound wisdom and discretion;
>   let them not escape from your sight,
> and they will be life for your soul
>   and adornment for your neck.
> Then you will walk on your way securely
>   and your foot will not stumble.
>   —3:21-23

> The beginning of wisdom is this: Get wisdom,
>   and whatever you get, get insight.
> Prize her highly, and she will exalt you;
>   she will honor you if you embrace her.
>   —4:7-8

Defining "Wisdom"

There have been numerous attempts to define precisely the concept of "wisdom" as that movement has developed in societies from the beginning of human history. It has been difficult to place a specific definition on the phenomenon, however, because there are so many different facets that comprise its totality. In the ancient world, for example, the term "wisdom" could refer to many different things. It could designate an accumulation of knowledge or factual data which, if one possessed the content of it, would make a person "wise." (Modern society understands the idea in much the same way.) Further, wisdom could refer to special skills or talents that enabled persons to accomplish duties or tasks in a successful manner.

Superior intellectual capacity could also qualify a person as "wise," but sometimes certain other intangible gifts were considered part of the total wisdom complex. For example, certain persons had the unique ability to discern hidden values or to estimate people at deeper levels than external circumstances might warrant or to ascertain where certain actions or attitudes might lead. Persons who possessed the special gift of "cunning" were considered "wise" also. Because all of these capabilities fell under the general category of "wisdom," it is easy to understand, therefore, why one definition will not contain all the various components that the ancients (and even moderns) understood to be part of the wisdom complex which enables human beings to cope with the world and even learn to use that world for their own good and/or pleasure.

The gift of wisdom, however defined, did not necessarily have any moral or religious connections, especially in its earliest stages. In most societies the wisdom movement gradually did become associated in some way with the religious ideas, beliefs, and practices of the particular culture from which its emerged. For example, there were flourishing wisdom traditions in the ancient societies in Egypt and Mesopotamia that reflected certain of the religious teachings of those cultures.[1] It will become clear shortly just how religious traditions influenced the development and growth of the wisdom movement in Israel and how that religion was, in turn, influenced by the wisdom movement.

The Two Directions of the Wisdom Movement

The wisdom movements in most societies developed in two directions. The first and most basic was the more pragmatic or practical type that consisted primarily of short proverbs containing instructions on how best to get along in this world. This took the form of wise sayings of parents to children or of teachers to students. The basic ideology underlying such an approach was that there is in this world a certain order and pattern; if one could learn to recognize and put this information to use, this learning would ensure a good and prosperous life for the wise person who follows the rules and regulations which are part of the world in which life is staged.

Examples of such thinking can be found frequently in proverbial teachings.

> He who is steadfast in righteousness will live,

[1] For discussions of these movements see James L. Crenshaw, *Old Testament Wisdom: An Introduction* (Atlanta: John Knox Press, 1981), especially pp. 212-235; R. B. Scott, *The Way of Wisdom* (New York: Macmillan Inc., 1972); and James Wood, *Wisdom Literature: An Introduction* (London: Gerald Duckworth & Co., Ltd., 1967).

> but he who pursues evil will die.
>> —Proverbs 11:19
> A perverse man will be filled with the fruit of his ways,
>   and a good man with the fruit of his deeds.
>> —Proverbs 14:14

The second type of wisdom arose and developed because, obviously, the first type is not always true. Persons who attempt to live by the "right" rules are not always rewarded with a good life; and those who callously flaunt the rules for living, rather than falling into an evil life, may prosper much more than those who follow the rules for right living. This observation gave rise to a more speculative or contemplative type of wisdom that attempted to understand why such situations occur and to answer further questions about what sense life really makes anyway.

Job in his suffering makes the following statement:

> Look at me, and be appalled,
>   and lay your hand upon your mouth.
> When I think of it I am dismayed,
>   and shuddering seizes my flesh.
> Why do the wicked live,
>   reach old age, and grow mighty in power?
>> —Job 21:5-7

Both approaches, though often seeming to be quite dissimilar, really were attempts to do the same thing—namely, to make some sense out of life and to find some order or pattern that would give meaning and purpose to the struggles a person encounters in this world. Wisdom is an attempt from the human perspective to subdue and master the environment so that a person can be ruler of life rather than seeming to be at the mercy of the powers of the world, which appear to be no respecters of persons or of neatly structured patterns.

The Wisdom Movement in Israel

Most studies of the wisdom movement in Israel point to the person of Solomon as the one who gave impetus to this phenomenon in Israelite thought. The Old Testament texts make this association (especially 1 Kings 4:29-34), and it is quite probable that the court of Solomon was the place where the first formal and sustained group of "wise men" flourished in Israel's history. This tradition was so strongly held that as history progressed, later generations all looked back to Solomon as the fount of wisdom and all wisdom was attributed to him. (Such a procedure was common in ancient Israel; often an entire movement was concretized in the person who began or popularized it. One recalls Moses and the Law and David and the Psalms as examples of this type of understanding.)

As important as Solomon was to the rise and development of wisdom in Israel, there are several other points that must be noted. The formal wisdom movements of the ancient world that developed a literature of their own were usually connected with court settings. They were part of the royal "machinery" that sustained the king and the state. One of the reasons, therefore, that wisdom did not flower until later in the development of Israelite culture is directly related to the fact that a monarchy was not established early in Israel's history and emerged only slowly and with resistance. If one wished, therefore, to locate the precise moment when wisdom became a formal part of Israel's environment, one would probably choose the time of the establishment of the monarchy under David, Solomon's father.[2] It remains true, however, that the Hebrew traditions maintained that the major emphasis on wisdom in Israel's history began with Solomon and his court.

The wisdom movement, after making a significant beginning under Solomon, became sidetracked because of the excesses practiced by Solomon and his court, which ultimately led to the split of the kingdom into northern Israel and southern Judah (around 921 B.C.). These circumstances did not exterminate the wisdom movement but did lead to a long period in which the "wise man" was present but not considered as one of the major forces in Israelite culture, especially Israelite religion. During this time another religious ideology held the field in Israel. This ideology had been partly to blame for the slow rise of the wisdom movement in Israel and became dominant again with the split of the kingdom.

Deuteronomic Theology

This ideology is usually referred to in scholarly circles as the Deuteronomistic or Deuteronomic theology, and its manifestations are found

[2]For an excellent discussion of this position, see Walter Brueggemann, *In Man We Trust: The Neglected Side of Biblical Faith* (Atlanta: John Knox Press, 1972).

most pointedly in the books of the Old Testament known as the Deuteronomistic history, for example, the books of Deuteronomy, Joshua (perhaps), Judges, First and Second Samuel, and First and Second Kings. This theology served also as the religious foundation for the teachings of the prophets, those men who felt themselves called by God to deliver God's Word to the people at particular moments of history. The basic idea within the Deuteronomic theology was very simple. If one obeyed Yahweh (the God of Israel) and Yahweh's laws, one would be rewarded with good life, protection, riches, health, and so forth; if, however, one did not obey Yahweh and Yahweh's laws, one would be punished. (The Deuteronomic theology had other components as well, but these are not really germane to the discussion here.)

One can already ascertain that such an ideology was quite similar to the basic teaching of practical wisdom, which taught that if one obeyed the laws of the world, one could have success and happiness, but if one disregarded those laws, one would have troubles and tragedies. The Deuteronomic religious ideology, therefore, was probably one of the major reasons why practical wisdom did not take its usual place as one of the great "molders" of society in ancient Israel as it had in other cultures. The same ideas were already there in theological dress, thus hampering the normal growth and development of this type of teaching in Israel. This is not to imply that practical wisdom did not exist in Israelite culture, for it certainly did, but the predominance of the Deuteronomic religious ideology hampered its growth into a full-blown and self-contained movement. The wisdom movement was given impetus under Solomon, but because of the breakdown of the kingdom as a result of Solomon's excesses, its development was delayed and it played "second fiddle," religiously speaking, to the Deuteronomic ideology, especially as that theology was embodied in the prophetic movement.

It is necessary at this point to pause and to comment upon a major item of Old Testament thought. The advocates of both the Deuteronomic theology and practical wisdom understood that the rewards and punishments which they described would take place *in this life*. The reason for this belief lay in the fact that in Old Testament thought there was no concept of an afterlife with rewards and/or punishments. For the Israelite people of that period, the beliefs concerning life after death centered in a place called *Sheol*. This was the name given to the place of the dead, a dark and gloomy realm where all people went upon death. There was no idea of annihilation in Hebrew thought, for each person in Sheol was still conscious, but existence there was the weakest kind of "life" one could imagine. This present life on earth was where real life was to be enjoyed and relished. It was in this life, therefore, that rewards and punishments were meted out. Once one went to Sheol, there was nothing but a dim shadowy existence; so this earthly life took on tremendous importance. The Deuteronomic theology and the practical wisdom ideology dovetailed neatly with this type of world view. These ideas are present in most of the Old Testament writings and did not die out easily. However, under the searching scrutiny of the later wisdom thinkers and even later with the development of apocalyptic thought, this type of understanding began at least to be questioned. More will be said about this in chapter 3.

Literary Types

To convey their ideas, the wisdom thinkers developed a simple and common-sense form of teaching device. The basic term used in Hebrew to designate such a presentation of ideas was *mashal*. It is very difficult to define this term precisely because various literary types and devices were included under the general rubric to convey certain teachings. Perhaps the best explanation of the term is to understand it as meaning "comparison." Teachings were conveyed in wisdom methodology by the use of short proverbs, pithy sayings, riddles, extended narratives—such as fables, allegories, or parables—poetic psalms, and so on. The use of any particular literary type was intended to cause the hearer or reader to reflect upon the truth contained in the teaching and consequently to challenge that person to compare the teaching to his or her own life and experience. This comparison elicited in the mind of the hearer or reader by the use of the *mashal* would, therefore, suggest some principle that could be used either generally or specifically to enhance the quality and understanding of life for the person who took the teaching seriously.

Early in the wisdom movement most of the *mashal* types were cast in the form of poetry. (This should give some clue as to how to interpret these teachings.) However, later in the postexilic period when the movement began to flower, a prose story form came to be used to convey ideas, meanings, and principles. This development will be discussed more fully as these later materials begin to emerge. For the moment, though, one must become acquainted with Hebrew poetry, for its patterns are somewhat different from modern patterns. One needs to recall, however, that poetry is not to be understood and interpreted in the same manner as narrative history. Ideas and principles are intended to be gleaned from such literary types; to interpret poetry literally is to miss the point of the author and to kill the spirit of the teaching.

Hebrew Poetry and Its Interpretation

Hebrew poetry differs somewhat from present-day poetry in that the basic characteristic of Hebrew poetry was not rhyme or rhythm but a structure known as *parallelism*. Since much of wisdom literature is written in poetic form (as well as the prophetic writings, the Psalter, and many other passages incorporated within prose tracts), it is essential to understand the nature of this literary phenomenon. Hebrew poetry is characterized by a structure in which the first line makes a statement to which is attached a second line that relates to the first line in one of three ways. First, the second line may restate the meaning of the first line; this is called *synonymous* parallelism. In the second type, the second line may state the opposite or a contrast to the first line; this is called *antithetical* parallelism. And finally, the second line may build upon and expand the meaning of the first line; this is called *synthetic* parallelism.

Naturally there were elaborations on these basic motifs, but these three simple types constituted the fundamental structure for the poetic literature in Israel. Illustrations of the types of poetry may serve to clarify the classifications. (These illustrations are taken from the Psalms.)

Synonymous:

> O LORD, rebuke me not in thy anger,
> nor chasten me in thy wrath.
> —6:1

> Set a guard over my mouth, O LORD,
> keep watch over the door of my lips!
> —141:3

Antithetical:

> O let the evil of the wicked come to an end,

but establish thou the righteous. . . .
—7:9

for the LORD knows the way of the righteous,
but the way of the wicked will perish.
—1:6

Synthetic:

O sing to the LORD a new song,
for he has done marvelous things!
—98:1

Arise, O LORD! Confront them, overthrow them!
Deliver my life from the wicked by thy sword. . . .
—17:13

It will be of great assistance to the interpreter if one is able to recognize poetry when it occurs and then remembers to interpret it as poetry. Mistakes in interpretation are frequently made when someone attempts to make literal history or extract literal meaning from poetry (after all, who really thinks that mountains break forth into song or that trees clap their hands, as written in Isaiah 55:12?). Understanding this is especially important when dealing with wisdom literature since most of this literature is conveyed in the poetic form.

Parable, Allegory, and Hyperbole

Just as poetry is not to be understood literally, neither are many of the other literary types that were utilized by the wisdom teachers. Perhaps the most familiar of all these types was the *parable*. The simplest definition of a parable is that it is a story taken from everyday life used to establish a point. The exact truth of the story was not a factor in determining the meaning of the parable. Such stories could be short or long, the longer ones (as indicated earlier) probably evolving later as the wisdom movement developed. The reader or hearer of the parable was challenged to find the point of the story and to act according to the truth contained therein. For example, the famous parable of the good Samaritan (Luke 10:29-37) has only one major point: Anyone in need is to be treated as one's neighbor, and to act on that need is considered appropriate (see the discussion of the parable in chapter 6, under "The Wisdom Method and the Teaching of Jesus").

Another literary type sometimes used by wisdom teachers was the *allegory*. Here the interpreter would find a story in which the author intended the hearer or reader to distinguish a hidden meaning for each item or character in the story. The intended identifications in such stories are usually either self-evident or explained so that the message of the author will not be misunderstood. All too frequently persons attempt to make allegories out of parables. Thus one must be cautious in dealing with these two literary types among the wisdom teachings. The major point to be emphasized again is that these are *stories,* told to illustrate principles or ideas; the absolute truth or falsity of the stories, historically speaking, has nothing to do with the validity of the points of the stories. This will become obvious when we examine some specific examples shortly.

One additional element must be kept in mind when dealing with wisdom literature, especially as it was found in the Semitic world. Quite frequently in that culture, teaching was expressed by the use of *hyperbole,* in other words, teaching by exaggeration. So permeative was this motif that one finds it used not only in short sayings but in longer stories as well. One illustration will suffice at this point to demonstrate how hyperbole was used. Jesus taught that "If your eye causes you to sin, pluck it out. . . . And if your right hand causes you to sin, cut it off . . ." (Matthew 5:29-30, and a similar saying in Mark 9:43-47). It does appear obvious that this saying was not intended to be taken literally, since all human beings, if they followed this specific direction, would be blind and without hands! The point of the saying appears simple enough: anything that stands between a person and God must be done away with, and quite frequently this process requires drastic action. No more should be made of the saying than that—but no less either!

The Riches of Wisdom Literature

What is found when investigating any wisdom movement, then, is a combination of practical observations about life, experiential information about the world one has to deal with, blended together with the thought patterns and culture of a particular people. These ideas and observations about life were preserved and transmitted by certain literary types, some in short sayings and some in longer story form. The wisdom teacher usually emphasized the individual as an individual, a human being attempting to cope with the world. Basically, wisdom attempts to teach that human beings in this world are both free and bound and that the wise person will learn to distinguish which aspects of life are which.

Not all the wisdom books deal with the same aspects and problems of life, but all of them do attempt to give direction to humankind for dealing with life and coping with the world. The direction of this study is now turned to the wisdom books of the Old Testament and to the wisdom method and teaching incorporated in the sayings of Jesus. If one understands something of the literary methods used by the wisdom teachers, these books take on much deeper meaning and significance. They truly give direction for persons who are attempting to cope with this world in its variety of challenges and ambiguities.

TWO

Coping When Things Are Normal

As is true with most wisdom movements, the earlier wisdom teachings in Israel tended to be more secular in nature than those that came later. It is quite probable that practical proverbial wisdom had been a part of Hebrew culture from the earliest times, but as already noted, the Deuteronomic theology delayed the full development of practical wisdom in Hebrew thought and its inclusion in the religion of the Hebrew people. Slowly but surely, however, this literary genre became a significant component of the religious traditions of the Jewish people.

Preliminaries to the Book of Proverbs

Practical and proverbial teachings probably became more directly linked with the religion of Israel when the fact was understood and clearly accepted that Yahweh was the God of creation. Since God had created the world as it was, with its laws and regularities and principles, it was believed that learning about these matters must be another way of learning about God. Therefore, living in accordance with the observed order of creation must be a part of living in obedience to God's laws.

As this principle was accepted, practical wisdom became more and more an integral part of Hebrew religious faith. The many proverbs collected together into the book of Proverbs are adequate testimony of this. Delayed in its full development by the older Deuteronomic theology, practical wisdom nevertheless overcame that obstacle to become a major component of postexilic Judaism.

The book of Proverbs as it now exists is in reality a collection of practical wisdom sayings gathered from a wide variety of backgrounds and time periods. All these have been placed in a religious setting which affirms with great conviction that

> The fear of the LORD is the beginning of knowledge;
> fools despise wisdom and instruction.
> —Proverbs 1:7

The collection of proverbs makes an attempt to direct the reader or listener away from danger and grief and toward happiness and comfort. The primary emphasis in these teachings is that certain rules exist in this world and in this life which, if followed, will ensure a good, happy, and prosperous existence; but which, if ignored, will mean ruin, shame, and unhappiness. The goal of life is, therefore, to learn the wisdom that holds the key to coping with the world. One must keep in mind, however, that the basic presupposition for such a philosophy is a regular and tranquil environment. In short, the emphasis of teaching with proverbs is upon coping with the world when all other things are normal.

The book of Proverbs probably did not take final form until later in the postexilic era. Scholars differ as to the date of the completion of the final editing process, but sometime around 300 B.C. would not be far from wrong. As one studies the book, it becomes evident that there are basically seven different collections which have been brought together to constitute the book in its present form. Some of the collections are very old, perhaps dating back to the time of Solomon; some reflect a long period of development both in style and thought, which causes scholars to locate them much later in the postexilic age (after 538 B.C.).

It would be virtually impossible to comment on each proverb contained in the book of Proverbs without developing a lengthy book. Several very good books already exist (see Suggestions for Further Study), and most of the proverbs are quite clear in their intention and meaning. Our discussion, therefore, will be limited to pointing out the various collections that comprise the book, commenting on the major themes and characteristics found in the collections, and examining several short passages to illustrate significant points.

The First Collection

Chapters 1–9 of the book of Proverbs contain the first major collection of teachings included in the book. The reader is immediately faced with a problem: Is the passage 1:1-7 an introduction to this collection only, or does it serve the larger purpose of introducing the entire book? There are some scholars who argue for each position. The technicalities of that discussion need not be reviewed at this point, but it seems likely that the passage was originally the introduction to the smaller collection. The final editors, however, placed this collection first since its introduction was appropriate for the larger work. Therefore, these verses seem to serve a double duty—an introduction to the smaller unit as well as to the whole book.

One notes with interest that these sayings were attributed to Solomon. It is quite possible that some of the proverbial sayings did indeed go back to Solomon and/or the wise men in his court, but it is not necessary to claim that all of these proverbs originated in that time and place. The reader is reminded of the Moses-Law and David-Psalms analogies described in chapter 1 under ''The Wisdom Movement in Israel.'' Since Solomon was the one who gave official status to the wise men, all wisdom according to the thinking of that time could be traced back to Solomon.

The purpose for the expounding of proverbs and for passing along such wisdom was to make it clear that this wisdom was both practical and religious.

> That [people] may know wisdom and instruction,
>   understand words of insight,
> receive instruction in wise dealing,
>   righteousness, justice, and equity;
> that prudence may be given to the simple,
>   knowledge and discretion to the youth—
> [that] the wise man also may hear and increase in learning,
>   and the man of understanding acquire skill. . . .
>
> —1:2-5, paraphrased

Here one finds the blending of Hebrew wisdom and religion without any thought that the two areas are in any way mutually exclusive.

As for the first major collection (1:8–9:18), scholars are agreed that this was the latest (in other words, the most recent or closest to our time) collection incorporated into the book of Proverbs. In this collection there is evidence of Greek thought and influence (something that did not come to this area of the world until the time of Alexander the Great, around 330 B.C.), and the sayings were written in a form that developed later in the wisdom movement. The basic style of these proverbs consists of somewhat longer poems that usually reflect certain themes, and they are set in the context of a father teaching his child or a teacher instructing students.

The most prominent topics of the teachings deal with the blessings of following a life of wisdom (2:1-22; 8:1–9:6), the folly of not adhering to the way of wisdom (9:7-18), and strong warnings against association with evil people (1:8-19; 3:27–4:27; 6:1-19). There are also specific warnings to young men to beware of evil women (5:1-20; 6:20–7:27). In each case, following the ways of the wise will assure one of a good and happy life, while ignoring these wise precepts will bring calamity and ruin. An illustration or two will suffice to demonstrate the flavor of the collection.

> My son, be attentive to my wisdom,
>   incline your ear to my understanding;
> that you may keep discretion,
>   and your lips may guard knowledge.
> For the lips of a loose woman drip honey,
>   and her speech is smoother than oil;
> but in the end she is bitter as wormwood,
>   sharp as a two-edged sword.
> Her feet go down to death;
>   her steps follow the path to Sheol;
> she does not take heed to the path of life;
>   her ways wander, and she does not know it.
>   —5:1-6

> Happy is the man who finds wisdom,
>   and the man who gets understanding,
> for the gain from it is better than the gain from silver

and its profit better than gold.
She is more precious than jewels,
   and nothing you desire can compare with her.
Long life is in her right hand;
   in her left hand are riches and honor.
Her ways are ways of pleasantness,
   and all her paths are peace.
She is a tree of life to those who lay hold of her;
   those who hold her fast are called happy.

—3:13-18

Happy is the man who listens to me [Wisdom],
   watching daily at my gates,
   waiting beside my doors.
For he who finds me finds life
   and obtains favor from the LORD;
but he who misses me injures himself;
   all who hate me love death.

—8:34-36

The Second Collection

The second of the collections, 10:1–22:16, in all probability contains some of the oldest sayings found in the entire book of Proverbs. Whereas the collection of chapters 1-9 has themes and groupings of proverbs dealing with similar issues, the structure of these chapters consists in a presentation of individual proverbs that are usually isolated and self-contained. It is interesting that they were attributed to Solomon. Since it is the consensus of scholarship that many of these are preexilic and very old, it may well be that many of them were, in fact, from Solomon or the wise men of Solomon's court. It is interesting also that there are 375 of these maxims, and that the word "Solomon" in Hebrew (adding the numerical equivalents of the letters of the name) totals 375! Most of the teachings in this second collection have to do with the contrast between the good life and the evil life.

He who walks in integrity walks securely,
   but he who perverts his ways will be found out.

—10:9

The righteous is delivered from trouble,

and the wicked gets into it instead.

—11:8

Whoever loves discipline loves knowledge,
but he who hates reproof is stupid.

—12:1

Misfortune pursues sinners,
but prosperity rewards the righteous.

—13:21

A soft answer turns away wrath,
but a harsh word stirs up anger.

—15:1

Wine is a mocker, strong drink a brawler;
and whoever is led astray by it is not wise.

—20:1

A good name is to be chosen rather than great riches,
and favor is better than silver or gold.

—22:1

As one can readily see, these proverbs are short, two-lined poetic sayings, self-contained and to the point. They reflect a very practical approach to life and the basic idea that if one does what is right, is industrious and responsible, one's life will be happy and successful.

The Third Collection

This collection, 22:17–24:22, contains, as the superscription says, "words of the wise." There are thirty proverbial poems in this grouping, many of which parallel an Egyptian work entitled *The Wisdom of Amenemope*. In terms of both content and pattern, there are definite connections between this Egyptian work and the collection under consideration here. Exactly how this came to be is not certain, but it illustrates that wisdom was a universal movement in the world of that time. Perhaps wisdom groups even shared materials. The teachings in this collection were directed primarily toward those persons who happened to be in apprenticeship for a career in public life.

Do not rob the poor, because he is poor,
or crush the afflicted at the gate;

for the LORD will plead their cause
   and despoil of life those who despoil them.
—22:22-23

Do not speak in the hearing of a fool
   for he will despise the wisdom of your words.
—23:9

A wise man is mightier than a strong man,
   and a man of knowledge than he who has strength. . . .
—24:5

These are basically practical proverbs that urge proper conduct and restraint, especially in public places, for persons in positions of authority.

The Fourth Collection

This is a second (and short, 24:23-34) collection of the "sayings of the wise," with a particular emphasis on the perils of laziness. The admonition to work hard is clearly seen in all these verses, and the following selection illustrates quite pointedly the essential teaching of the collection.

A little sleep, a little slumber,
   a little folding of the hands to rest,
and poverty will come upon you like a robber,
   and want like an armed man.
—24:33-34

The Fifth Collection

Some very old material is also contained in this section, 25:1–29:27. The heading reads, "These also are proverbs of Solomon which the men of Hezekiah king of Judah copied" (25:1). That some of these sayings are very old (the collection may be from around 700 B.C.) is indicated by the fact that chapters 25–27 contain the most secular of all the proverbs. Chapters 28–29, however, are more religious in tone and outlook, and so they may come from a somewhat later time.

The early chapters basically give advice on how to cope with the world in such a manner as to ensure avoiding trouble, especially in human relationships.

Like clouds and wind without rain
   is a man who boasts of a gift he does not give.
                                        —25:14

Let your foot be seldom in your neighbor's house,
   lest he become weary of you and hate you.
                                        —25:17

He who meddles in a quarrel not his own
   is like one who takes a passing dog by the ears.
                                        —26:17

A prudent man sees danger and hides himself;
   but the simple go on, and suffer for it.
                                        —27:12

In the later chapters one finds a much stronger emphasis on the place of God in one's life and an emphasis on morality as such rather than simple pragmatism as was the case in chapters 25–27. These chapters, 28-29, are simply more religious than 25–27.

Evil men do not understand justice,
   but those who seek the LORD understand it completely.
                                        —28:5

A greedy man stirs up strife,
   but he who trusts in the LORD will be enriched
                                        —28:25

Bloodthirsty men hate one who is blameless,
   and the wicked seek his life.
                                        —29:10

An unjust man is an abomination to the righteous,
   but he whose way is straight is an abomination to the wicked.
                                        —29:27

The Sixth Collection

This section, 30:1-33, is entitled "The words of Agur son of Jakeh of Massa." There is considerable debate about the unity of these verses. Some scholars treat the chapter as basically from one source, while others find divisions within the chapter from several sources. Some interpreters divide the material into 30:1-10 and 30:11-33; others make the division differently—30:1-14 and 30:15-33; still others break it down even further. The sources are not of great import for our purposes, however, and will not be discussed further.

The underlying theme of the majority of the sayings incorporated in this chapter seems to be that of moderation, keeping to a middle ground in one's attempt to live in this world. Extremes lead one into trouble; avoid them!

> Remove from me falsehood and lying;
>> give me neither poverty nor riches;
>> feed me with the food that is needful for me,
> lest I be full, and deny thee,
>> and say, "Who is the LORD?"
> or lest I be poor, and steal,
>> and profane the name of my God.
>> —30:8-9

The latter portion of the chapter is filled with several numerical proverbs, another popular type of wisdom form.

> Under three things the earth trembles;
>> under four it cannot bear up:
> a slave when he becomes king,
>> and a fool when he is filled with food;
> an unloved woman when she gets a husband,
>> and a maid when she succeeds her mistress.
>> —30:21-23

The Seventh Collection

The last collection, chapter 31, bears the superscription "The words of Lemuel, king of Massa, which his mother taught him." It appears, however, that this title may refer only to vv. 1-9, which give direction as to how one can be a good leader. The other material, 31:10-31, is an acrostic poem extoling the value of a conscientious wife and mother. Even in a male-dominated society, as this definitely was, it was recognized that a good wife and mother was a person worthy of considerable respect and esteem.

> A good wife who can find?
>> She is far more precious than jewels. . . .

Charm is deceitful, and beauty is vain,
but a woman who fears the LORD is to be praised.
—31:10, 30

Summary

In these various collections many topics were discussed by the ancient writers or collectors. These topics dealt with most aspects of life in this world and attempted to direct the young and the unlearned in the ways by which one could bring more success and stability into one's life. In some respects the reading is somewhat monotonous, for the book of Proverbs deals with the everyday, sometimes humdrum, concerns of daily living, but these concerns were vitally important to people attempting to make the most of what all too often seemed to be a confusing and harsh existence. It may well be, therefore, that the practicality of the wise men who compiled this book spoke more directly to the needs of the people than did all the liturgies and sacrifices of the priests and all the thundering ideals of the prophets! This literature gave people some specific directions for the living of their lives.

Coping When Tragedy Strikes

Whereas the practical wisdom contained in the book of Proverbs spoke to the human struggle to cope with the world, that philosophy basically required a normal life setting, a situation in which all other things are equal. It is a fact of human existence, which one can learn simply by observing life as it really is, that there are many moments in the lives of individuals or groups or nations when things are not equal. Goodness, industry, and trust in God do have their rewards, but unfortunately there are times when life falls in upon a person for no apparent reason, certainly not because that person (or group) has sinned. How does one explain these occurrences? What about suffering that is undeserved? Or what about the wicked whose lives are easy?

The great United Kingdom of David and Solomon had split into two smaller entities, Israel and Judah (around 922/921 B.C.). Both nations had been warned by the prophets that unless they returned to Yahweh with proper contrition and unless they kept the requirements of Yahweh's covenant with them, they would be punished. The ax fell on Israel in 722/721 B.C., and the people were carried off into exile never to return, just as the prophet Amos had announced. Not having learned any lesson from Israel, the nation of Judah continued on its wayward path. Finally, in 597 B.C. and 586 B.C. the nation of Babylonia defeated Judah twice and carried many of its people into exile.

Unlike the people of Israel, who were scattered by the Assyrians over the Mesopotamian area, the people of Judah were taken into Babylonia and kept rather close together. When Cyrus the Persian defeated the Babylonians in 539 B.C., he decreed that captured peoples could return to their homelands. This included the people of Judah. Some of them returned to Judah in 538 B.C., but they found the situation there very harsh. The prophets had told them that their punishment was a result of their sin (typical Deuteronomic theology) but that the punishment had passed. The time supposedly was right for restoration, not simply in terms of a return to the land, but in terms of prosperity and a new and glorious political kingdom. However, neither prosperity nor statehood came for many years. The people suffered both individually and collectively.

During the postexilic period, therefore, when the historical fortunes of the Jewish people were at this very low ebb, people of sensitivity began to wrestle with and attempt to make sense of the seeming incongruities of life. Why did industry and faithfulness fail to guarantee success? From these struggles came the books of Job and Ecclesiastes, which some interpreters have labeled "speculative" or "philosophical" wisdom. This type of wisdom was represented in other cultures as well, most notably in Egyptian and Babylonian writings, but it did not emerge in Israel's history in advanced form until after 400 B.C. Most probably such speculation emerged directly from the historical plight of the people of Judah in these troublesome times. The old Deuteronomic theology and the basic ideas of practical wisdom simply did not explain the realities of their existence at that time and place. These were good people who suffered unjustly while evil persons who lived lives of luxury and plenty and immorality escaped without ever having to "pay the piper." It was at this moment of history that the time was right for the development of speculative wisdom in Hebrew thought.

Introducing the Book of Job

Almost from the beginning of human history, the plight of the truly good person who suffers greatly has been a puzzle to persons of sensitive and thoughtful character. We find stories of "righteous sufferers" in very ancient literature (for example, in Egypt and Babylonia), but as long as the Deuteronomic religious thought pattern prevailed in Israel's religious thinking, there was little room for this kind of speculation in Israel. The proverbial wisdom, while it recognized that some good people do suffer at times, usually interpreted undeserved suffering as a means of testing one's faith and/or as a means of strengthening one's faith and character. The Deuteronomic thought pattern emphasized the corollary idea that if one were being punished, that person or group had definitely committed some sin for which punishment was specifically *deserved*.

Out of the historical setting of the postexilic era came a sensitive thinker who attempted to speak to the depressing situation of the Jewish people. The author of the Book of Job used an ancient story about a righteous person who encountered horrible calamities and then supplemented this basic, traditional story with poetic dialogue in order to speak to the nation during that period of harsh conditions. In fact, the author probably used several different sources in the composition of this book but blended them together into a marvelous story. The scene was set in the patriarchal age (the times of Abraham, reflecting how old the basic tradition was) and the hero was not an Israelite, even though he did worship Yahweh. Scholars are not in absolute agreement as to the date of the book in its final form, but the majority of them place it somewhere in the postexilic period. The best conjecture would perhaps be somewhere between 400 and 300 B.C.

Precautions and Problems

There are several points to be remembered as one studies the Book of Job. The interpreter must keep in mind that the Hebrew text of the book has not been preserved as well as one might have desired. This fact means that at several places in the book it is very difficult to translate the text with any confidence. There are points at which one can only conjecture what the exact meaning may have been. Usually, however, the general theme or emphasis is fairly clear, even though the exact wording may not be.

A second consideration is partially related to the first. As one studies the development of the Book of Job, it becomes clear that at certain places there have been some editorial revisions. Whether these resulted from the fact that the text was in less than perfect condition, whether these revisions *caused* the textual problems, or whether some other explanation may provide a more appropriate solution of this problem is not known. It is clear, for example, that in the third cycle of the dialogue between Job and his friends, the structure of the passage has been altered; whether it was done deliberately from the first or because of some textual problem later (for example, the destruction of a part of the manuscript) cannot be determined.

There are two other passages that also cause scholars difficulty. At the conclusion of chapter 31, Job issued his audacious challenge to God to appear—or else! In chapter 38 God did exactly that, but between the two chapters one finds a rather long discourse by a certain Elihu, who does not appear either before or after this portion of the book (chapters 32–37). Most scholars think that these chapters were added to the book later since they appear to interrupt the flow of the story and because the language and style are different from the language and style of the remainder of the book. A suggestion will be offered shortly as to why the final editors included these chapters, but it seems obvious that they were not a part of the initial version of the Book of Job.

Another problem revolves about chapter 28. This chapter contains a magnificent hymn in honor of wisdom, but the religious ideology of the poem is rather typical of the practical wisdom thinkers (thus very close to Deuteronomic theology). In its present position in the text, the poem is placed on the lips of Job. This puzzles interpreters because if Job, at this point, had believed what the poem espouses, the remainder of the book would have been superfluous. In fact, if Job had believed the contents of this poem, none of the book would make any sense! Therefore, many scholars have argued that this chapter was inserted into the text at a later date. The problem with this theory is that the poem is obviously in the language and style of the writer of the other poetic sections of Job (except the Elihu speeches), and it is generally agreed that this passage came from the pen of the original poet. It will be contended in this discussion that the poem is where the author originally placed it. The interpretation of this chapter and its place in the flow of the story will be discussed more fully in the exposition of the book. It is sufficient to mention here that there is a problem with the interpretation of the chapter in its present context, however.

The purpose of the writing of the Book of Job has often been misunderstood. Some have argued that the main purpose was to answer the question "Why do the righteous suffer?" Others have proposed the problem of theodicy, or the justice of God: Why does God allow evil and injustice to exist in the world? Even though these particular motifs are included and discussed in the writing, answers to these questions are not to be found; therefore, answering these problems cannot be postulated as the primary reason for the writing of the Book of Job. Perhaps it would be best to examine the book itself before making a judgment as to the real purpose of the author in composing this majestic piece of literature.

When trying to classify the type of literature into which this writing fits, some have argued that the book was intended as a drama. Others have suggested that this was an epic; still others, a dialogue. Some like to think of the book as an enlarged parable. It is probably impossible to catalog this work precisely, for the author has taken an ancient folk tale and expanded it through his own poetic genius into the moving religious story that has spoken to many people in all ages of human history. Perhaps the great scholar R. H. Pfeiffer has caught something of this when he writes: ". . . we may regard it as one of the most original works in the poetry of mankind . . . it is not exclusively lyric . . . nor epic . . . nor dramatic . . . nor didactic . . . or reflective . . ."[1] Even though it defies exact specification in terms of type of literature, the book is definitely inspired and inspiring! The major thought to keep in mind is that the book is basically a *story,* a literary device used to convey meaning, which is typical of the wisdom movement in many cultures. The fact that it is a story should not bother the modern interpreter, especially if one understands the wisdom method of presenting ideas and truths. (Some persons, for example, are quite relieved when they understand this point and learn that God did not capriciously "roll the dice" with Job's life.)

Job's Story

The book itself can be outlined very easily into five distinct parts.

Outline of the Book of Job
I. Prose Introduction: 1–2

[1]R. H. Pfeiffer, *Introduction to the Old Testament* (New York: Harper & Row, Publishers, Inc., 1948), p. 684.

II. Dialogue Between Job and His Friends: 3–31
III. Elihu's Speeches: 32–37
IV. Yahweh's Answer to Job: 38:1–42:6
V. Prose Epilogue: 42:7-17

The Prologue

The Book of Job begins with a prose prologue (chapters 1–2), which probably had a long and ancient tradition attached to it. The purpose of this prologue is to set the stage for the struggles of Job as they will be unfolded to the reader. Job is a genuinely righteous man. He is also very wealthy by human standards. He is depicted as a man of integrity, a concerned father, and a truly righteous human being. He is not a Jew; rather, he is depicted as being a native of the land of Uz (probably in Edom, but this is uncertain).

The scene suddenly changes from earth to the very throne of Yahweh. It appears that the beings in the court of Yahweh are gathered to give an account of themselves in terms of their assigned duties. The reader is introduced here to the figure of the "Satan," the "Adversary" in Hebrew. Satan is mentioned only a few times in all the Old Testament writings. In most of these places he is a being in the court of God whose duty is to search out the evils of human beings and report those evils to God (see Zechariah 3:1-2). In one place (1 Chronicles 21:1) he appears as one who attempts to provoke or tempt humans to sin. In any case, Satan is not yet depicted as the epitome of evil, the leader of the forces of demonic powers, and the ultimate symbol of sin and rebellion against God that he becomes in the intertestamental period.

Yahweh, obviously annoyed at how much Satan is able to "dig up" about human beings, takes some consolation in the fact that at least Job is truly a righteous person. But Satan challenges God on this point. "Does Job serve God for naught?" Satan argues that it is profitable for Job to be righteous and God-fearing. If Job were not rewarded, perhaps he would not be so inclined to be religious. God, therefore, allows Satan to test Job. The *reader* of the story now knows why Job is going to suffer. The characters of the drama, just as people in life, do not.

Now, after a quick series of catastrophes, Job is informed that he has lost all that he has (except for his wife!). His material possessions are stolen and destroyed, and his children (his link to the land of the living, as well as his pride) are killed by a tornadolike wind. All these events are told to him in rapid-fire order. At this point, however, Job still retains his basic trust in God and speaks those well-known words associated with him, "Naked I came from my mother's womb, and naked shall I return; the LORD gave, and the LORD has taken away; blessed be the name of the LORD" (1:21).

Again the scene shifts to the heavenly court. Yahweh asks Satan for the second time, "Have you considered my servant Job . . . ?" (2:3). Satan now argues that the tragedies have not really "hit home" since nothing has happened directly to Job himself. To this charge God responds by allowing Satan to inflict harm on Job's body. The wager continues.

What the exact ailment was with which Job was afflicted is not known, but some scholars have proposed some form of elephantiasis common in the East. Such a disease was a form of leprosy, which was a sign of God's displeasure in that culture and which also had direct religious connotations (see Leviticus 13:1-46). This may explain Job's sitting on the ash heap *outside* the town or village, since lepers were considered as being cut off from the community of God's people.

When Job's friends from distant places hear of his misfortune, they come to visit him, making an arrangement to meet together, which indicates that Job has been on the ash heap for some time. The purpose of their visit is to comfort Job. They do not recognize him at first, probably because his features are very distorted. They sit with him in silence for seven days and seven nights, the designated time to mourn the dead. At this point the prose gives way to magnificent poetry, which continues throughout most of the book.

A Dialogue of Arguments

The structure of the second section (chapters 3–31) appears to have been composed as a dialogue between Job and the three friends. After Job introduces his problem in a lengthy opening discourse (3:2-26), there follows a series of speeches by the three friends, each of which is responded to by Job. In other words, Eliphaz speaks, Job responds; Bildad speaks, Job responds; and Zophar speaks, Job responds. This sequence is followed precisely in the first two cycles (chapters 4–21), but in the third cycle (chapters 22–28) there appears to have been some textual displacement and later editorial revision. It is possible that part of the original text was lost from this section, thus causing the problems mentioned previously. An attempt will be made shortly to reconstruct this last cycle.

The content of this larger section (chapters 3–31) depicts Job arguing his innocence of wrongdoing in the face of his three friends, who adhere to the party line that anyone suffering must be guilty of sin.

The First Cycle

After the opening statement by Job lamenting his present predicament, cursing the day of his birth (very close to cursing God, if not actually the same!), and longing for death to release him from his agony, the discussion begins with Eliphaz carefully but pointedly suggesting to Job that the reason for his suffering must lie in some sin.

> "If one ventures a word with you, will you be offended?
>   Yet who can keep from speaking? . . .
> Think now, who that was innocent ever perished?
>   Or where were the upright cut off?
> As I have seen, those who plow iniquity
>   and sow trouble reap the same."
>
> —4:2, 7-8

He further argues that Job should welcome this chastening so that Job can be strengthened by it.

Job responds with a more determined inquiry, however.

> "Teach me, and I will be silent;
>   make me understand how I have erred."
> —6:24

His suffering is great and is described rather vividly (7:5). Even in sleep Job cannot find respite from the agony. He longs for death and does not want to live out his alloted days (7:13-16). This was a quite startling conclusion for someone in those days, for death cut one off from the potential joys of life. There were no rewards or punishments after death, only the gloomy existence in Sheol (see the discussion of Sheol under "Deuteronomic Theology" in chapter 1, "Introduction").

As the dialogue continues, it becomes more personal and more bitter. Bildad, for example, suggests that Job's children died because they deserved that fate (8:4). Zophar chastises Job because he refuses to admit his legitimate guilt. "Know then that God exacts of you less than your guilt deserves" (11:6c). After these charges in the first cycle, Job responds to his "comforters,"

> "No doubt you are the people,
>   and wisdom will die with you"
>   —12:2

Job's plight raises the question about the concept of life after death held in that day. If indeed, as was believed, the good are rewarded here in this life and the evil receive their just due, fairness and justice are served. Job, however, now knows that this scheme is not true to human experience. This theological doctrine, wrapped neatly with the "bow of orthodoxy," does not fit the realities of human existence. Things in this life do not always even out. Such a situation is patently unfair, Job argues.

> "For there is hope for a tree,
>   if it be cut down, that it will sprout again. . . .
> Though its root grow old in the earth,
>   and its stump die in the ground,
> yet at the scent of water it will bud
>   and put forth branches like a young plant.
> But man dies, and is laid low;
>   man breathes his last, and where is he? . . .
> If a man die, shall he live again?"
>   —14:7-14a

Of course, the answer to that question in Job's mind and in his culture was a resounding *no*. There was no theological theory or teaching that could answer the question of justice and fairness in this world. Some people do suffer unjustly. Tragedy is real in the realm of human existence. The wisdom thinkers of the postexilic period gave impetus to the discussion and development of ideas concerning life after death. This discussion arose from the frustration that the Jewish people were feeling in their grinding struggle to survive in the midst of a cruel and sometimes hostile environment. Some of this questioning and thinking is reflected in the struggles of Job.

The Second Cycle

The discussion between Job and the three friends becomes more and more bitter. Job says, ". . . miserable comforters are you all" (16:2b).

He insists even more strongly that he is innocent of any wrongdoing
that would warrant the degree of suffering he is experiencing. This
certainty leads to one of the most famous of the quotations from the
book of Job. Unfortunately, however, most persons have not understood
what the saying really meant to convey. The passage in question is
found in 19:23-29, expecially verses 23-27. Attempting to interpret this
passage correctly is difficult because this is one of the places where the
text seems to have been corrupted. The exact translation, especially of
verses 26-27, can be, therefore, only a conjecture. Further, one must
understand the meaning of the Hebrew word *go'el* (usually translated
"redeemer") if any proper interpretation of the passage is to be possible.

The figure of the *go'el* in Hebrew culture related to the whole concept
of justice and making things right in this world. The word *go'el* basically
indicated a vindicator or avenger. For example, if a person had been
wronged or harmed, it was the duty of someone, usually a close kinsman, to avenge the wrong done to that person. If a person's good name
or character had been besmirched, the *go'el* was to clear that person's
name of the damage done to his or her character. One finds numerous
examples of this type of thinking and action in various Old Testament
texts (see Numbers 35:12; 2 Samuel 14:11; and so forth). What Job is
saying in this passage is that he is so certain of his basic innocence that
he believes someone, somewhere, someday, will clear his name of the
charges brought against him by the three friends, who were only reflecting what others were thinking about Job.

Job believes that he will be acquitted of any wrongdoing that deserves
such severe suffering, but he has given up hope that it will be before
his death. The translation of verses 26 and 27 is very uncertain because
of the condition of the Hebrew text. Probably it should read something
like this: ". . . after my skin has been thus destroyed [in other words,
after his death], then [apart] from my flesh I shall see God [?], whom
I shall see on my side. . . ." Several things should be kept in mind.
Job is not arguing here that he will have some sort of life after death
wherein he will be rewarded. This idea has already been rejected (see
14:7-22). He is, however, definitely protesting his innocence and obviously feels that the only one who can truly act as his *go'el* is God.
Family and friends have all deserted him (19:13-19); his suffering is
so great that only God can vindicate such implied evil. Job is therefore
asserting a strong hope ("faith" is probably too strong a word for this

setting) that God's justice will ultimately prove him innocent of any charges of evil that deserve the suffering that he has experienced. His good name is at stake; his innocence has to be established—only God can do that!

Zophar responds (chapter 20) by reiterating the certainty that evil is punished. To that neat theological answer Job replies (chapter 21) by insisting that this argument lies shattered on the rocks of reality.

"How then will you comfort me with empty nothings?
There is nothing left of your answers but falsehood."
—21:34

The debate is becoming more and more heated.

The Third Cycle

In the third of the cycles (chapters 22–28), the reader will find some confusion with regard to the speeches and to the speakers. There must have been some textual problems in this section of the manuscript which caused later editors to attempt to reconstruct some of the speeches and to determine who said what in this sequence. For example, as the text stands, Job sometimes delivers two speeches in succession; Bildad's speech is very short; and Zophar has none at all! Added to these peculiarities is the problem of the possible insertion of the famous hymn to wisdom (chapter 28). The third cycle seems to be rather garbled.

It is the position of this writer that the third cycle must be modified in order to make sense of the text, but with as little rearrangement as possible. The speech of Eliphaz in chapter 22 and Job's response in chapters 23–24 are complete as they stand. The speech of Bildad in chapter 25 is exceedingly short, however, and in 27:1 one reads, "Job again took up his discourse." Why is this necessary if he has just spoken in chapter 26? It seems best, therefore, to delete the statement in 26:1 indicating that this is Job's response and to understand 26:2-14 as a continuation of the speech of Bildad. This appears likely since these verses seem to consist of sarcastic barbs directed at Job, who (the friends think) considers himself wiser than he should. Job's response to this speech is then found in 27:1-6.

It is at this point that part of the text seems to have been either destroyed or lost. Job's speech seems to have been cut short, for beginning with 27:7 there is the continuation of another speech from one of Job's friends. Since Zophar is not mentioned at all in this last section, it appears reasonable that this is his speech. Thus, one can surmise that the conclusion of Job's speech and the beginning of Zophar's speech are missing.

Chapter 28, as the text now stands, is placed on the lips of Job. The problem is that the poem in honor of wisdom does not fit the mind-set of Job at that moment. Scholars, as already noted, tend to take this poem as a later insertion into the original Book of Job, even though in form and content it appears to have been written by the author of the book. Various theories have been espoused, but none is universally accepted. Certainty cannot be reached, and unanimity among interpreters will probably never be found. It is the opinion of this writer that the poem is by the author of the original Book of Job and was indeed a part of the original work. The tragedy is that because the text of this section is in such bad repair, our attempts to make sense of this portion of the book are seriously hampered.

The solution offered here is that this chapter was intended as the concluding argument of the three "comforters." Whether it was intended as the concluding remarks of Zophar's last discourse or as a separate summary cannot be known with certainty. Most commentators agree that these words are simply not appropriate on the lips of Job. If he had believed these things, there would have been no reason for the discussion with the friends and no need for God to speak to him from the whirlwind. The statement in chapter 28 is exceedingly orthodox in regard to the position of the three friends and should be understood, therefore, as their concluding statement.

In chapters 29–31 Job then delivers a final analysis from his position. He protests his innocence, even enumerating all the sins he can think of that could have produced this grave tragedy. Finally the possibilities are exhausted, and Job issues a final ultimatum to God. "Come here! Tell me *why?!* And do it *now!*"

A Young Man Speaks

At this point in the development of the story one would expect some kind of response from God to Job's near blasphemy. Instead, the reader encounters a series of four speeches (chapters 32–37) by a certain Elihu, a younger man, who has not been mentioned before and is not mentioned afterwards. These speeches are not responded to by Job, and neither do they seem to add anything to the development of the ideas contained in this book. Most scholars are convinced that these chapters are a later insertion into the final edition of the Book of Job. In fact, the language and style of the writing point to a different author.

The speeches of Elihu do, however, reflect some understanding of the discussions that have gone on between Job and his three friends. Elihu attempts to summarize the situation to this point and to show how each side is wrong. He believes that suffering is for discipline and that discipline cleanses a person from sin and guilt. (But it is interesting to note that Eliphaz has already argued this point. See 5:17-27.) What the later editor meant to accomplish by inserting these chapters, therefore, is not really clear. Elihu does emphasize that wisdom is to be found in God and that God is above the finite and puny minds of humankind, but these ideas, too, have already been argued (chapter 28).

The final redactor or editor of the Book of Job must have felt that some purpose was served by the inclusion of this Elihu section into the narrative. The purpose is not obvious, however, to most modern interpreters, but one could conjecture that the final editor believed that there was error on both of the sides of the argument up to this point and wanted to emphasize that. This, then, would prepare the reader for the speech by Yahweh and the final resolution of the situation which occurs in chapter 42 (about which more will be said later) after Job's confrontation with God. Further, another point could be that God does not respond immediately to threats or harangues, such as Job had delivered, from human beings—even suffering human beings.

The Answer from the LORD

The reader now reaches the climax of the book. Job's challenge to God, issued at the conclusion of chapter 31, is finally accepted. God speaks to Job from the midst of the whirlwind.

Interpreters differ in their assessment of these chapters. As the chapters are now structured, Yahweh speaks to Job in 38:2–40:2; at this point Job speaks only briefly, 40:3-5. Yahweh then continues to speak, beginning with much the same words as in 38:2; this speech continues to 41:34. Job again makes a short statement (42:2-6), at which point the poetic body of the book ends.

Some scholars speculate that there may have been some disarrangement of the text in these chapters. It appears that 40:15–41:34 are

perhaps secondary and were a later addition. Some, therefore, structure
Yahweh's speech as 38:2–40:2 followed by 40:7-14. This would mean
that Job probably answered only once and that Job's reply to God is
found in 40:4-5 and 42:2-6. These passages were probably together
originally but were separated when the insertion of 40:15–41:34 was
made. Whatever the solution to this problem, it is clear that the meaning
of these chapters is essentially the same, no matter what disposition is
made of the arrangement of the text here.

Yahweh appears to Job but does *not* answer or even speak to Job's
questions nor to the "wisdom" of the three friends. There is no discussion of justice, righteousness, reward or punishment, good or evil;
there is only the revelation of God in overwhelming majesty and creative
power. Through this revelation Job learns just how little he understands
or can ever understand about God or the world!·

> Then Job answered the LORD:
>
> "Behold, I am of small account; what shall I answer thee?
>   I lay my hand on my mouth.
> I have spoken once, and I will not answer;
>   twice, but I will proceed no further."
>
> —40:4-5
>
> " 'Who is this that hides counsel without knowledge?'
> Therefore I have uttered what I did not understand,
>   things too wonderful for me, which I did not know.
> 'Hear, and I will speak;
>   I will question you, and you declare to me.'
> I had heard of thee by the hearing of the ear,
>   but now my eye sees thee;
> therefore I despise myself,
>   and repent in dust and ashes.''
>
> —42:3-6

It is in these verses that the climax of the book is reached. Job at
this point finally understands that there are things in this life and in this
world that can never be understood or explained. He was not told why
the righteous suffer, or why a good God allows evil in the world God
created, or why justice seems to be perverted, even thwarted. What Job
learns is that knowing this God is the greatest and most important thing

that any human being can hope for. To know God in the biblical tradition means to experience the reality of God's presence in one's life. This cannot be taught or found by searching in theological orthodoxy or passed from one person to another; it must be experienced intimately and personally. When Job received a glimpse of the greatness of this God, all else seemed to pale into insignificance.

Even though Job did not discover why he was suffering, he learned something far more valuable. In spite of suffering (even in spite of prosperity and good times), one can experience the presence of God and have fellowship with God. All other matters are secondary when viewed against that understanding.

The Epilogue

The reader now comes to the prose epilogue that forms the final section of the book. It is interesting that these verses presuppose not only the first two prose chapters but the content of the poetic section (3–31, 38:1–42:6) as well, indicating that even though several sources may have been used by the author of Job, the book as it stands is basically a unity.

There are some interpreters who feel very uneasy with these last verses. The great lesson that Job has learned, namely that one's relationship with God is the most important aspect of life and that this can continue in spite of the worst that the world has to offer, seems to be contradicted by Job's having his prosperity returned. Is not this what Job originally thought, and what the three friends were arguing? Has the author become a Deuteronomist or forgotten his powerful point? Various attempts to explain this problem have been forwarded, but perhaps the most simple, as well as the most logical, is the explanation postulated by the great English scholar, H. H. Rowley. He argues that the fortunes of Job were restored, not because Job had been found righteous, but because the trial or period of testing was over. To have left Job in his state of misery would have been an ". . . expression of God's arbitrary malice. . . . "[2] The author did not wish to leave this kind of impression about the character of God, even in a story. After all, this was a dramatic *story* written to illustrate a great religious truth. Job had learned the greatest lesson of religion: one's relationship with

[2]H. H. Rowley, *New Century Bible Commentary on Job,* rev. ed. (Grand Rapids: Wm. B. Eerdmans Publishing Co., 1976), p. 343.

God is not based on material externals. The restoration of his fortune was, for all practical purposes, therefore, irrelevant.

It is also interesting to note that Job's fortunes were not restored immediately, however, but only after he carried out a command by God. That command directed that Job offer sacrifices for his three "comforters" who "have not spoken of me what is right, as my servant Job has" (42:8). Such a surprising statement placed on the lips of God is somewhat distressing to some people. After all, the three friends had tried to defend God against the increasingly bitter Job. It was Job who cursed the life God had given to him, who implied that God was not just or did not care (perhaps did not even know) about Job and his plight, who accused God of doing this evil to him, and who dared God to face him. Such behavior surely could not be accounted as right! What meaning could the author have had in mind?

It appears that what is being advocated is for persons to speak of God as they have experienced God personally. As human beings we cannot understand everything that occurs in this world; therefore a person has to adhere to a sense of integrity and honesty. One cannot affirm something that he or she has not experienced and should not be dogmatic in the face of others' experiences. Pat theological doctrines that have not been tested against the abrasive realities of the world are of little, if any, value! Job, in spite of all his bitterness and carping, maintained a kind of integrity that obviously found favor before God; he spoke of and held to that which he knew to be right, in this case his own innocence. He was unwilling to compromise his integrity for theology. He learned that religion—relationship with God—is more important than theology—theories about God; one's relationship with God is more important than what may be happening to a person at any given moment.

Who was, after all, right about Job—Satan or God? One recalls the wager between the two in chapters 1 and 2. Most commentators agree that God (who else?) was right about Job, and ultimately God's trust in the basic integrity of Job was found to be correct. But Satan also was right about Job; it *was* profitable for Job to be religious. And even though Job did not actually curse God, he came as close as anyone could—and perhaps even did curse God (see chapter 3). In reality both Satan and God were correct, Satan at the beginning but God ultimately. However, Job was a different man at the conclusion of the book; here was a Job who had "seen" God and was properly overwhelmed by what he had learned about God.

The Lesson from the Book of Job

The author of the Book of Job was truly inspired. He produced a masterpiece of religious insight and some of the most majestic poetry of the entire Old Testament. The interpreter must keep in mind that this "story," told in the wisdom tradition, was meant to raise questions about and offer a solution for the suffering of the people in his times. Such a marvelous message is certainly applicable in analagous situations today in the lives of both individuals or groups who have experienced staggering tragedy. The lesson of Job is not that evil will go away or that the righteous will ultimately triumph or that God acts in certain ways and dares puny mortals to question these ways. The lesson Job learned is that relationship with God, real religion, can sustain one no matter what the external situations may be. Perhaps two quotations may help in summarizing the message of this book:

> For tortured spirits theology is less satisfying than religion, and religion is encounter, encounter with God. It is in the sphere of religion rather than in theology that the meaning of the book is to be found. . . . [Job] felt himself shut out from the presence of God. A false theology sapped the springs of religion, when religion was most needed. . . . It is of the essence of its message that Job found God *in* his suffering, and so found relief not *from* his misfortunes, but *in* them . . . . the message of Job . . . is that here and now in the fellowship of God the pious may find a peace and a satisfaction that transcends all the miseries of his lot.[3]

> The poem of Job ends on a central biblical truth: if God is to be known he must make himself known and no amount of talking about him can replace the reality of his presence or the void of his absence. . . . As for the purpose of suffering, the book of Job offers several suggestions but no dogma. Suffering may be retribution, testing, discipline, or it may in the end be largely inexplicable. What matters is the purity of one's relation with God, unadulterated by the circumstances of success or failure.[4]

[3]*Ibid.*, pp. 19-21.

[4]Norman K. Gottwald, *A Light to the Nations: An Introduction to the Old Testament* (New York: Harper & Row, Publishers, Inc., 1959), p. 485.

FOUR

Coping When Life Makes No Sense

The book of Ecclesiastes is in some ways one of the most intriguing of all the books in the entire Bible. That it is unorthodox, when judged against most of the other biblical writings, is the consensus among interpreters. The book is permeated by a large dose of skepticism and seeming despair, and it is rather well known for these characteristics. Who has not heard that famous quotation from Ecclesiastes, "Vanity of vanities, all is vanity"? Many interpreters have understood this famous line as the key to understanding the basic teaching of this book. As a result of the seeming despair diffused throughout this writing, the book had a difficult time being accepted. There was much debate among the rabbis as to whether it should be accorded a place among the sacred writings, and it was only by a narrow margin that the book was included in the canon. Even today many persons shy away from the document because they feel that it is too depressing and negative in its outlook. If one examines the book carefully, however, one finds that there is a much more positive message than a superficial reading may suggest.

The person whose sayings are collected into this book was probably a teacher in a school for the wise in Jerusalem. He appears to have occupied a place among the elite and privileged of his time. Even though he is loosely identified with Solomon (not surprising in wisdom circles) in the first two chapters, that identification is not pursued in the remainder of the book and was probably utilized in chapters 1 and 2 for literary rather than historical reasons. That he was held in high esteem can be clearly seen in 12:9-10, an appendix to the book that was probably added by one of his students.

The author is known by the name Qoheleth (pronounced *Ko-hél-eth*). In Hebrew this title possibly denotes someone who speaks to an assembly. The term "Ecclesiastes" is the Greek equivalent of the Hebrew title, and it is from the Greek that we receive the name of this biblical book. The idea that the function which this title designated was that of addressing an assembly has led to the more popular appellation for the author—"the Preacher."

Dating this writing has engendered considerable debate among scholars. All things considered, however, the most probable time for the final editing seems to have been the middle of the third century B.C., around 250. There is really nothing in the contents of the book itself that gives any clue for linking some specific historical occurrence with this document. The date, therefore, is derived from certain linguistic and philosophical criteria that emerged later in the postexilic era.

A Guide to Discussion of Ecclesiastes

As for an outline of the book, many scholars have agonized mightily, attempting to find some kind of clue that would give to this writing some semblance of unity and order. But, alas, there is none to be found. Most interpreters simply acknowledge that the book is a loose collection of sayings and reflections about life from "the Preacher," without any real inner order or cohesion. Many different outlines of the book have been suggested, and the one presented here is given basically to assist the reader in following the discussion of the contents of this book.

Outline of the Book of Ecclesiastes
   I. Introduction: 1:1-11
  II. The Search for Meaning in Life: 1:12–3:15
 III. Observations on Life: 3:16–9:12
  IV. Virtues of Wisdom: 9:13–11:8
   V. The Joys and Challenges of Youth: 11:9–12:8

VI. Editorial Additions: 12:9-14

Qoheleth, perhaps more than any other biblical thinker, attempted to be *realistic* about life, depicting it, not as we would like for it to be or as it ought to be or even as the orthodox religious teachings of his time taught that it was, but as it really is. He began with his observations on life, his experiences with life, and his speculations about life's meaning. Does life actually have any meaning? If so, how or where? Can one be happy in the midst of such a world as ours? If so, how or where? Can one find any direction for the living of life? If so, how and where? These musings form a collection of reflections on life that attempt to make some sense out of this nonsense we often call "our existence." Basically Qoheleth struggled to combine the regularity of life and the world with the ambiguities and inconsistencies one encounters in life and in this world. He tried to hold these two components together in some way so as to make sense of everything. He did not really succeed in this attempt, but his struggle may be helpful to any who will follow along with him in his reflections.

Human Attitude Creates Despair

The first few verses of Ecclesiastes set the tone for the entire work.

> The words of the Preacher, the son of David, king in Jerusalem.
> Vanity of vanities, says the Preacher,
>   vanity of vanities! All is vanity.
> What does man gain by all the toil
>   at which he toils under the sun?
> A generation goes, and a generation comes,
>   but the earth remains for ever.
> The sun rises and the sun goes down,
>   and hastens to the place where it rises.
> The wind blows to the south,
>   and goes round to the north;
> round and round goes the wind,
>   and on its circuits the wind returns.
> All streams run to the sea,
>   but the sea is not full;
> to the place where the streams flow,
>   there they flow again.

All things are full of weariness;
  a man cannot utter it;
the eye is not satisfied with seeing,
  nor the ear filled with hearing.
What has been is what will be,
  and what has been done is what will be done;
  and there is nothing new under the sun.
Is there a thing of which it is said,
  "See, this is new"?
It has been already,
  in the ages before us.
There is no remembrance of former things,
  nor will there be any remembrance
of later things yet to happen
  among those who come after.

—1:1-11

The first verse is, of course, a superscription or title that was probably placed here as an introduction to the book as a whole and that connects this wisdom teacher with Solomon. This connection is quickly abandoned, however.

Verses 2-11 introduce the reader to the problems to be examined. When one thinks about the world as it is, realistically, apart from any religious or theological consideration, there seems to be no rational explanation for what occurs in life. There is some regularity in the world and for that one can be grateful, but that same regularity can at times become simply monotonous, resulting in a feeling of futility in life that deadens one's interest in and motivation for living.

There may be in these verses, however, a much deeper meaning than is sometimes acknowledged. Is Qoheleth pessimistic simply because of the monotony of nature, or could it be that the problem lies in the human dimension in life? Are the regularities of life a curse in and of themselves, or is it that human beings fail to see the positive elements in this regularity and to take advantage of the situation? He says, "What has been done is what will be done. . . . Is there a thing of which it is said, 'See, this is new'? It has been already in the ages before us" (vv. 9-10). Qoheleth may be acknowledging that human beings have not really learned from their past, have not taken advantage of opportunities offered, and that human nature, being what it is, will probably never learn from its mistakes. This situation is truly a cause for despair, but it derives from the human attitude toward life, not from fixed or predetermined negativities. The problem lies within human beings. The enemy is "us"!

The Frustration of Discontent

The first major section of the book (1:12–3:15), therefore, depicts Qoheleth as imagining that he is Solomon, king of magnificent wealth and wisdom. Such a setting is perfect for presenting his struggles with the question of exactly how one finds positive meaning and purpose and satisfaction in life. One searches for these elusive goals through the accumulation of knowledge but finds that the more knowledge one acquires, the more depressing life can become. One can learn about the intimate secrets of life, but one also learns just how little one can really understand in spite of accumulated knowledge. I knew a college professor who defined education as a "series of disillusionments"; it seems that Qoheleth had much the same idea years before:

> For in much wisdom is much vexation,
>   and he who increases knowledge increases sorrow.
>   —1:18

The search for meaning in life is continued by the author's depiction of someone's being immersed in extreme pursuits for pleasure. The description presents a picture of almost total hedonism, but that, too, is found to be futile and meaningless. The search then shifts to the accumulation of fame and power that are depicted as increasing beyond imagination. That also is found meaningless.

One of the reasons for Qoheleth's ultimately negative conclusion on these issues arises from the recognition that when one does accumulate wealth and wisdom, these are then left to someone who has not worked for them—and the implication is that the one to whom these are left neither deserves them nor appreciates them nor knows how to use them! The primary point seems to be that there is no long-term, abiding contribution that can be assured. Pleasure also has no lasting effect. The problem is the future. Can it be changed for the better?

Commentators have had great difficulty with 2:24-26:

There is nothing better for a man than that he should eat and drink, and find enjoyment in his toil. This also, I saw, is from the hand of God; for apart from him who can eat or who can have enjoyment? For to the man who pleases him God gives wisdom and knowledge and joy; but to the sinner he gives the work of gathering and heaping, only to give to one who pleases God. This also is vanity and a striving after wind.

Some argue that these verses should be understood as sarcasm—life should be this way, but it is not. Others have postulated that a later editor added this passage to make Qoheleth sound more orthodox. Neither of these explanations make sense in the light of the fact that the entire section concludes with another "vanity" statement. It appears that Qoheleth's observation here is that although God acts in certain ways to give life meaning, life unfortunately still does not make sense to him! This passage dramatically reflects the tension between the positive and the negative aspects of life as presented in Qoheleth's musings. The positive note here is that when one does find enjoyment in life, this should be understood as a gift from God. Even so, however, life continues to remain a mystery in its larger context.

Included at this point the reader now finds a short poem that is quite well known in our present society.

For everything there is a season, and a time for ever matter under heaven:

a time to be born, and a time to die;
a time to plant, and a time to pluck up what is planted;
a time to kill, and a time to heal;
a time to break down, and a time to build up;
a time to weep, and a time to laugh; . . .
a time to keep silence, and a time to speak;
a time to love, and a time to hate;
a time for war, and a time for peace.

—3:1-9

The gist of this poetic piece seems to be that (1) there is an appropriate moment in life for all of a person's most significant life events; (2) there is a certain regularity in the way the world operates; and (3) there is a certain inevitability about the events of life. Qoheleth has again faced the realities of life and has found both positive and negative aspects in them. He teaches clearly that God has created the world, but he is not sure how God remains related to it since there are so many uncertainties and inconsistencies in the midst of the regularities.

In verses 10-15, which conclude this segment, the argument is presented that somehow God *intends* for humankind to find enjoyment and happiness in life and in life's work. Yet even here human inability to comprehend the totality of existence is affirmed: ". . . [God] has put eternity [some translators read "obscurity"] into man's mind, yet so that he cannot find out what God has done from the beginning to the end" (v.11).

The curious statement in verse 15, "God seeks what has been driven away," probably refers to the cyclical nature of the world and the recurring events of life as Qoheleth has viewed them already in 1:2-11 and in 3:1-9. These are positive aspects of life not negative aspects as humans sometimes understand them.

A Collection of Observations

Beginning at this point in the book (3:16), there follows a long selection of sayings that basically deal with the injustice and unfairness that are prevalent in the world. Intermingled with these negative musings are statements that tend to be positive in nature, but there seems to be little, if any, real structure in the thoughts presented.

Qoheleth has looked for justice and righteousness in the very places where one expects them to be—in the law court and in the temple—but alas could not find them there. He affirms that God will ultimately set things aright, but he immediately remembers that such a conclusion cannot be demonstrated.

Qoheleth also appears to be puzzled by the seeming reality that human beings are ultimately of no more significance than the animals. He believes that human beings must be of greater value than the dumb beasts, but who can really say that the one is more highly "called" and therefore more valuable than the other? This seems to be the meaning of verse 21, "Who knows whether the spirit of man goes upward and the spirit of the beast goes down to the earth?" This verse actually raises a question about creation. Are human beings really made in God's image, and are they really the crowning point of the created order (see Genesis 1:26-31)? One may sincerely believe that humans are more valuable in God's plan of things than other creatures, but is this provable? (This verse should not be interpreted as an attempt to depict rewards in an afterlife, as some have argued. Qoheleth believed, as did the author of Job, that Sheol awaited each person.)

The argument now moves to another topic with little or no real organizational structure with regard to the order of the matters discussed. First of all, Qoheleth asserts from his observations that the world is not as it should be (see 4:1-3). For example, there are times when the oppressed and powerless people of the world have no one to assist them. When such situations occur, the dead are the lucky ones—but even more fortunate are those who have never been born and so have never seen the evil of the world or tried to make sense of it!

The reader, at this point, encounters a series of descriptions of meaninglessness in life, resulting from the peculiar mixture of good and evil in the world. Even good things in this world all too often stem from evil motives. "Then I saw that all toil and all skill in work come from a man's envy of his neighbor" (4:4). The sage does believe, in a positive vein, that when people work together, there can be strength and mutual assistance for each separately and the group collectively (4:9-12).

Another curious and difficult saying is found in 5:8-9:

> If you see in a province the poor oppressed and justice and right violently taken away, do not be amazed at the matter; for the high official is watched by a higher, and there are yet higher ones over them. But in all, a king is an advantage to a land with cultivated fields.

This puzzling expression again seems to imply that in this world there are both positive and negative elements. Rulers, even though one may find unjust and oppressive ones, are necessary for an orderly structure in life. A good ruler is an advantage and is worth the risk one takes of getting a bad one.

There is also a large section (5:10–6:12) that deals basically with the futility of the accumulation of wealth. The person who loves money will never get enough; in fact, the more one has, the more one worries about losing what has been accumulated. What really counts is for one to find real satisfaction, enjoyment, in the work one does irrespective of the financial gain. Qoheleth argues that a person who is unable to enjoy what is available would have been better off to have been aborted before birth, but then with his usual ambivalence Qoheleth raises further questions. With our limited knowledge and understanding, who among us really knows exactly what is good for us in this world? Who knows how our actions may or may not affect the future? And is not this, the possibility of affecting the future, more important than material gain?

At this point in the writing a poem is included (7:1-13) in which it is suggested that some things in this world are better than others. One is surprised to find that most of the *better thans* are basically negative. Qoheleth seems here to espouse the principle "Look at the gloomiest side and perhaps things won't be as bad as one expects!" Life must be taken seriously and one must accept life as it comes, the good and the bad, though it would be nice if all of life could be positive and constantly filled with joy.

The reader now encounters a rather lengthy and loosely connected series of sayings (7:15–9:6) which upon first examination seems not to hang together. Upon closer examination, however, a theme does appear to be present, binding the segments together. The central idea focuses upon the seeming inequities in life—the difference between what is and what ought to be. For example, the righteous are not always blessed, nor the evil punished. Such reality discourages persons from even wanting to attempt to be righteous and makes the search for a truly good person a difficult task. Qoheleth despairs of finding even one good woman in a thousand! People are basically selfish and therefore evil, but it is interesting that this cynical sage still believes, in spite of the fact that it cannot be proved, that the wicked will not ultimately prosper (8:13).

Qoheleth has raised a question similar to one raised by the author of the Book of Job concerning the fate of persons after death. "This is an evil in all that is done under the sun, that one fate [Sheol] comes to all . . ." (9:3). It just does not seem right to Qoheleth that the same fate comes to the good man, who has integrity, and the evil man, who lives deceitfully. Against the backdrop of such penetrating questioning by the wisdom thinkers about this topic, a doctrine of life after death eventually began to evolve in the religion of Israel. Qoheleth, however, did not progress beyond the old ideas about Sheol.

The statement of Qoheleth that most nearly characterizes his positive view of life is found at the conclusion of this section: ". . . a living dog is better than a dead lion'' (9:4*b*). The basic thrust of the ancient sage's thought remains: there is hope in life, in being alive, in the struggle against the evils of the world, in the struggle to make sense of it all. ''Where there's life, there's hope'' seems to be his basic watchword, for when death comes, the struggle for enjoyment or for good or for understanding is over.

The short passage 9:7-12 seems to complete the thought of the preceding section. *Enjoy life* as best you can. But remember that not always the most qualified or deserving person is rewarded the most. Luck enters into the picture as well (''. . . but time and chance happen to them all'' [v. 11*b*]). And it is a fact that no one knows when the moment for death will come.

Wisdom and the Worth of the Struggle

The next section of this book (9:13–11:8) consists of a loosely knit collection of sayings extolling the virtues of wisdom, in spite of the fact that neither wisdom nor the wise man is often heeded in this world. The reason for this last phenomenon is that (according to Qoheleth) there are many people who are lacking in even the most elementary rudiments of wisdom! People act in ways that are disastrous and continue to do so, never seeming to learn from their folly. They have not profited by the lessons of the cyclical and regular nature of life, which should serve as valuable instruction for living in this world.

The basic focus of the sage remains—*keep on trying* even in the face of uncertainty. ''Cast your bread upon the waters for you will find it after many days'' (11:1). *Keep on hoping* in spite of the fact that ''. . . the days of darkness will be many'' (11:8*b*). One can never really make sense of all of life, but the struggle is worth the effort! There is a sense of satisfaction and reward in the struggle, in having played the game of life to the fullest, in having tried to make life better and to make sense of it.

The Vitality of Youth, Plus a Word of Caution

The words of Qoheleth conclude with a challenge to young people to enjoy their youth (11:9–12:8). Obviously the teacher is now old and remembers with nostalgia the positive things he either enjoyed or missed in his earlier years; he covets for his students (and any who will hear) a full enjoyment of life at every stage. To a certain degree this admonition for youth to enjoy life is a modification of the usually accepted pattern of Hebrew society. In those days the period of youth was, to a certain extent, looked upon as a time of training to prepare for receiving the respect and admiration that would come only with age. It appears that Qoheleth sees some very positive possibilities in the young, aside from their vigor. He also cautions that what one does in youth will some day have to be paid for. "But know that for all these things God will bring you into judgment" (11:9c).

One of the most well known verses from this book is found in 12:1. It is also probably misunderstood because of a textual problem that has caused a mistranslation. The popular version reads, "Remember also your Creator in the days of your youth. . . ." The word "creator" was probably at first intended to be the word "grave." This reading fits the context much better. The Hebrew words are so similar that it is quite likely they were confused. The difference is between *bor'eka* (creator) and *bor^{e}ka* (grave). Verses 2 through 7 are usually interpreted as a graphic, symbolic description of what happens to a person in old age when the inevitable end of human life approaches.

When death comes, the human body returns to dust and the animating Spirit of God returns to God. This "spirit" should not be interpreted as the human spirit or the "soul" of a person. Life ultimately is a gift from God and when the end comes, the animating spirit that made life possible is returned to God. The personality, or soul, of the person went to Sheol, as Qoheleth has already made clear on several occasions. With this segment the teachings of Qoheleth are concluded (12:8).

Additions by the Editor(s)

Several additional verses have been added to the collection of this great sage's teachings (12:9-14). These verses, by almost unanimous consent, are from a later hand. How many "hands" have been at work here is not agreed upon, however. Some think that verses 9 and 10 were added by one editor, verses 11 and 12 by another, and verses 13 and 14 by yet another. Whether there were as many as three authors or as few as one, these last verses are editorial comments by someone else, possibly some of his disciples, about Qoheleth's teachings. It is obvious that this wise teacher was beloved by at least some, verses 9 and 10 making that point very clear.

There are several points that deserve mention with regard to these additional verses. For example, there are the curious words "The Preacher sought to find pleasing words, and uprightly he wrote words of truth" (12:10). Interpreters are somewhat puzzled about the exact meaning of the word "pleasing," however. The words of this book are not easy to hear or to reflect upon. At points they appear to be in contradiction, and to some sensitive souls they are downright depressing. How then can such words be pleasing? Probably we should understand the "and" in verse 10 as indicating the adversative conjunction "but." The meaning would then be that Qoheleth wanted to find easy solutions and pleasing answers to the mysteries of human existence, *but* because he had to be honest and follow the truth, he had to "tell it like it is!"

The saying in verse 11 is probably an apology for the note of despair that sometimes permeates Qoheleth's words, as well as an apology for the probing and questioning of traditional orthodoxy. The Deuteronomic theology and even practical wisdom teaching are basically rejected here as not conforming to reality. There is also a warning for other persons not to wander too far beyond the bounds of these sayings (v. 12); it takes a special kind of person to wrestle with such deep ideas without becoming overwhelmed by despair. It is best for most ordinary mortals to leave such speculation to those who are suited for this task by training and by nature, and to learn from their struggles.

The final two verses (13-14) in a sense summarize the entire teaching of Qoheleth, drawing out the most positive elements scattered throughout the meanderings of the teacher. Most commentators fail to see the very real and positive aspects of Qoheleth's thought, but his students understood the deepest feelings of their master. To keep on going in this world, doing one's duty in spite of the uncertainties and ambiguities of life with the hope that God, somehow, somewhere, will make things balance—this is the last summary of this marvelous man's thought. It seems to be exactly what he has meant throughout his sayings.

A Final Resting upon God

To be sure, the teachings of Qoheleth have many depressing notes in them, but, overall, if one looks closely, the message is basically positive, not negative. Qoheleth attempted to combine in an understandable package the regularity of life and the world with the ambiguities, uncertainties, and unfairness of life and the world. He tried to make sense of it all! After searching diligently, at great sacrifice to himself, he was honest enough to admit that he could not make all the pieces fit. He concluded that neither wisdom nor power nor wealth nor pleasure nor work can either separately or collectively explain the deepest meaning of life. The foundation for true meaning has to be located outside ourselves and outside the world. Otherwise all is "vanity and a striving after wind" (6:9b). Only God can give life meaning, and human beings are unable to fathom the mind of God. Basically this ancient sage had a very positive sense of God and God's inherent goodness. Even though Qoheleth did not like what he saw in this world and did not claim to understand life as it really is, he did not blame God for the situation (as had Job, for example). He believed that the proper attitude of human beings before God was awe and respect and trust (see 5:1-7). Qoheleth, as did all the other biblical writers in one way or another, rested his hope upon the God to whom he had committed his mind—and his life.

FIVE

Coping in Critical Situations

Even though the books of Proverbs, Job, and Ecclesiastes are the ones primarily designated as belonging to the wisdom genre among the Old Testament writings, it is probable that several others owe their existence to this movement as well. These are Ruth, Jonah, Esther, and possibly the Song of Songs. The first six chapters of the Book of Daniel also fall into the wisdom category. To understand why this literary grouping probably belongs to the wisdom movement, it is necessary to examine briefly some of the history of the postexilic times and to explicate a bit further the continuing development of the wisdom traditions.

As already indicated, the Jewish people had returned from Babylonia around 538 B.C. with high hopes and great expectations for the restoration of their community and their state. Unfortunately, the realities of life are quite frequently much more harsh and difficult than the idealistic expectations that persons envisage. Times were hard; politically, the Jewish people remained a subgroup within a larger Persian administrative district. They had no real protection from stronger and more established peoples in the area. When marauding armies crossed

Palestine, the Jewish community in Judah could offer no resistance to them.

In the midst of such harsh times these people struggled mightily to survive. One important development that greatly assisted their survival was the completion and acceptance of the Torah in its present form (as far as can be determined). This document became authoritative for the life and faith of this struggling community. Even so, times were so harsh that survival became problematic; therefore, to continue as a unique people and to preserve the traditions of their past, the community began to turn in upon itself and to become rather exclusivistic. Nehemiah and Ezra, for example, strongly discouraged any intermarriage with foreigners and even argued that any non-Jewish persons be expelled from the community, along with any children they may have had while married to Jewish people!

In this period of harsh political reality, difficult economic times, literary growth, and contemporary religious development, the community in Judah did its best to survive and to keep alive the ancient traditions. So far as can be ascertained, there were two major issues of importance: (1) What does the religious tradition require of us in this situation? and (2) What can we do to survive these troublesome times? As one can readily see, these two questions were integrally related.

Work on the ancient traditions produced the Torah and later the prophetic materials (the Former Prophets: Joshua through Second Kings; and the Latter Prophets: Isaiah, Jeremiah, Ezekiel, and the book of the Twelve Minor Prophets). These two bodies of materials preserved the religious heritage of the Hebrew people but also were edited in such a way as to challenge the people in their new situation. Religious development and thinking continued, however, and were not limited simply to the past traditions. The work of Ezra and Nehemiah triggered work on a new history of the community that scholars attribute to the work of the "Chronicler," the editor/author of First and Second Chronicles as well as the books of Ezra and Nehemiah. This historical account represented the more introspective and exclusivistic tendencies in this postexilic community.

Newer types of material and newer ways of thinking were developing in the area of the wisdom traditions. Some of the richness of this movement has already been dicussed in this book, centering in the books of Proverbs, Job, and Ecclesiastes. The wisdom movement and wisdom thinking were much more permeative than a study of these three books alone might indicate, however. The basic concept of *mashal* (comparison by short sayings, proverbs, or parable) to make a point began to be expanded in longer prose stories. One is reminded of the Book of Job, whose author took an ancient idea about a righteous sufferer and expanded it into a long story by the use of magnificent poetry. That tendency toward poetry, however, gave way to stories told primarily in prose form. Many stories can be found in those books that did not find a place in the Old Testament canon (for example, Judith and Tobit), but several such literary works were accepted as authoritative and were included among the sacred books of Judaism. These were Ruth, Jonah, and Esther.

One other book may also belong to the wisdom sphere—the Song of Songs. There is sometimes embarrassment expressed for the inclusion of this writing into the canon of sacred Scripture, because it deals with the sheer joy of human sexuality. It is generally classified among the wisdom writings, though some scholars dispute that categorization. The fact that the writing was attributed to Solomon may have tipped the scales in favor of wisdom, however.

Additional influences of the wisdom style can be clearly identified in other Old Testament books. For example, the story of Joseph found in Genesis 37–50 is now generally agreed to be the product of wisdom influence. The first six chapters of the Book of Daniel are obviously wisdom stories told to illustrate certain emphases which the people of that particular time needed to hear. In addition to these specific texts of some length, numerous shorter passages appear in various other books and reflect wisdom-type teaching devices. There are, for example, proverbial sayings in Jeremiah (2:22; 5:8; 13:23), numerical poetic passages in Amos (1:3–2:6), and hyperbolic poetry in Isaiah (40:2-5; 55:12-13). The list could be multiplied, but these examples suffice to demonstrate the permeative growth of wisdom in Israelite history.

In the postexilic era there were many wisdom teachings presented in various forms. The most popular form appears to have been the short story. It is to examples of wisdom teaching found in this form that our study now turns.

The Book of Ruth

As already indicated, the postexilic period was a time of constant struggle for the Jewish people in Judah. During this era they developed a definite tendency toward exclusivism, even to the point of dismissing their foreign spouses along with the children of these marriages. Many interpreters of the Old Testament believe that the story of Ruth developed as a reaction of protest against these extreme measures, especially those enacted during the reforms of Ezra and Nehemiah. Others think, however, that the book was simply intended as a source of hope and strength for the people who had returned from exile and were experiencing hard times. Whatever one wishes to do with the specific setting for the book, it remains certain that the story as it now exists sprang from wisdom circles.

Originally the nucleus for this story probably came from an ancient tradition that had been passed along through the centuries. There are some scholars, for example, who find in this story the remnants of a myth that was somehow connected with a fertility cult located in Bethlehem. Still others believe that the names of the characters were intended to have symbolic meanings. The book took final form, however, against the background of the postexilic era, and if one reads the story carefully, the book interprets itself as many of the wisdom teachings did.

Outline of the Book of Ruth

I. Introduction: 1:1-5
II. Tragedy and the Return of Ruth and Naomi to Judah: 1:6-2:23
III. Ruth Keeps the Levirate Law: 3:1-4:12
IV. Happy Ending for All: 4:13-22

The historical setting for the story of Ruth was during the period of the Judges. (This explains why the book, even though written in the postexilic period, came to be included in the Old Testament canon after the Book of Judges.) A certain Hebrew couple, Naomi and Elimelech, moved to the land of Moab with their two sons because of a famine in Judah. The two sons found wives for themselves among the young women of Moab. In the course of time the father and the two sons died.

Naomi, the mother-in-law of the two Moabite women, urged them to return to their families. One of them did so; but the other, Ruth, insisted on staying with Naomi and accompanying her back to Judah. It was she who spoke those famous words that are often quoted by starry-eyed lovers: "Entreat me not to leave you or to return from following you; for where you go I will go, and where you lodge I will lodge; your people shall be my people, and your God my God; where you die I will die, and there will I be buried'' (1:16-17*a*). The reader naturally notes with interest the emphasis in this statement by a non-Israelite woman that she wanted to be a member of Naomi's people and to be a devotee of the Hebrew God!

Upon returning to Judah the two women found life very difficult. Ruth went out into the fields to glean so that the two could survive. The law dictated that some of the grain was to be left in the fields and grapes in the vineyards for the poor (see Deuteronomy 24:19-21; Leviticus 19:9-10, 23:22). When the owner of the fields, a certain man named Boaz (who the reader learns was a kinsman of Naomi), saw Ruth, he inquired who she was. When he was told, he instructed Ruth to gather grain in his fields and strictly charged his workers not to molest her. (Is this perhaps a clue as to what happened to poor women in such conditions in those times?)

When Ruth reported to Naomi what had happened, the mother-in-law was astounded at their good fortune that Boaz was a relative. As the reader has already learned, in ancient Hebrew thought it was believed that all persons upon death went to a place called Sheol, that gloomy place of weak consciousness and existence. The ancients believed that if a link to the land of the living could somehow be retained through descendants, the gloomy existence of Sheol could be somewhat alleviated. This meant that it was a necessity for a person to have children to continue this connection to the land of the living. If a husband died without offspring, that was a grave tragedy. Therefore, the "levirate law" was established. This regulation dictated that it was the *duty* of the next of kin (usually a brother of the husband, although other relatives were also acceptable) to "visit" the widow for the purpose of impregnating her. The child born as a result of this union was considered the offspring of the deceased. At this point the woman could marry the father of the child, but such does not seem to have been an absolute necessity. Other children, if the couple did marry, were considered to be children of the living husband, but the first was the child of the deceased husband! (See Genesis 38 for an illustration of the law.)

Naomi instructed Ruth about this matter and sent her back to present herself to Boaz that very night! Ruth was to observe where Boaz slept, uncover his "feet" (probably a euphemism for genitals), and then do whatever Boaz told her to do. Having followed her mother-in-law's instructions to the letter, Ruth uttered these words when Boaz awoke: "I am Ruth, your maidservant; spread your skirt over your maidservant, for you are next of kin" (3:9, and this means exactly what it appears to mean!). To which Boaz replied: "May you be blessed by the LORD, my daughter. . . ." Boaz knew, however, that there was a nearer kinsman than he, but he promised Ruth to fulfill the law if the next of kin was not willing. The other kinsman preferred not to perform this duty because of inheritance complications (the child would not have been considered his but, rather, the child of Naomi's husband and sons; see 4:17).

To summarize the rest of the story rather quickly: Boaz obtained the right to fulfill the levirate law for Ruth; a son was born, and Ruth and Boaz were married. The important point that gives the story its major impetus appears to lie in the genealogy at the conclusion of the book. The child born to Ruth was named Obed, who was the father of Jesse, who was the father of David. The greatest of all the Hebrew rulers had Moabite blood flowing in his veins!

The point of the story is clear enough. Foreign people can become true and faithful worshipers of Yahweh; they can keep the laws of Yahweh. And when that occurs, Yahweh can bless them and the special people, Israel, through these faithful actions. This story may well have spoken to the postexilic community in Judah, which had become rather exclusivistic in its attitude and constituency. The Book of Ruth is a typical wisdom-type story told not simply to be entertaining and inspiring but, more importantly, to make a serious religious point. It does this very well.

The Book of Jonah

The Book of Jonah, while included among the prophetic books, seems to exhibit the characteristics of the wisdom-story form. It is unique among the prophetic books in that all the others primarily contain sayings of the prophets, along with a few historical accounts in some of the longer works. The Book of Jonah, however, is a story about a prophet from beginning to end.

Most scholars are agreed that the Book of Jonah, even though set in the preexilic period, was composed in its present form sometime during the postexilic period. The reasons for this conclusion seem to be quite justified. For example, the language and style of writing reflect postexilic, not preexilic, Hebrew. The description of the city of Nineveh (one of the great cities of Assyria) appears to reflect wisdom-type hyperbole rather than a straight historical account. To our knowledge Nineveh was never as large as the story indicates.

Further, the purpose for the writing of this book seems to be much better suited to the postexilic era than to the preexilic era. The nation of Assyria was a scourge to the people of antiquity. The records of its atrocities were boldly recorded in the documents that have been discovered among the ruins of that nation. Before Assyria's fall, therefore, in the time of the Babylonian Empire (around 612 B.C.), the primary attitude toward Nineveh and Assyria was one of utter disgust and hatred (see the book of the prophet Nahum). The message of the Book of Jonah becomes very pointed when one recalls that the postexilic community had become very exclusivistic, turning its back on the primary reason for its special status, which had been established by God's call to the Hebrew people to bless all nations (Genesis 12:3) and to be a light to the nations (Isaiah 42; 49:6). It appears, therefore, that the most appropriate historical setting for this writing lies in the postexilic Jewish community in Judah, and that the purpose was to call the people away from their extreme exclusivism and their negative attitude toward non-Jews.

The story of Jonah seems to be a *mashal,* a typical wisdom story told to challenge the hearers and readers to compare themselves with Jonah—and to compare their pagan neighbors with the people of Assyria depicted in the story.

Outline of the Book of Jonah
  I. God Calls Jonah to Preach to Nineveh: 1:1-16
 II. Jonah Swallowed by the Fish: 1:17–2:9
III. Jonah Proceeds to Nineveh and Preaches: 2:10–3:10
 IV. Nineveh's Repentance and Jonah's Response: 4:1-11

The delightful story of Jonah is told with wit and incisive humor. It moves quickly from scene to scene to make its point. The narrative begins abruptly with God's call to Jonah to go and preach to Nineveh—whereupon Jonah immediately bought a ticket on a ship bound for Tarshish (in Spain), the furthest point west known to the ancients in this area. Assyria, of course, lay to the northeast!

At this point the reader encounters the first of numerous circumstances that Yahweh "appointed." The Lord caused a great wind that threatened to sink the ship while Jonah lay sleeping peacefully in an inner compartment. As the sailors attempted to find some way to save the ship, the captain woke Jonah. Jonah told them who he was and that it was his fault that the storm had been sent. He instructed them to throw him overboard so that they could be saved. These pagan sailors, however, continued to struggle to save themselves *and* Jonah! Finally when nothing else seemed to work, they threw Jonah overboard, where a specially appointed fish swallowed him.

Interpreters have argued over a long period now about this great fish. Some have argued that it was an actual fish, and such persons try to find supporting evidence by searching for information about large fish species that could swallow a human being and/or about persons who have been swallowed by some fish and have lived to tell about it. Others argue that the fish was really symbolic and should be understood as a reference to the exile of the Hebrew people in Babylon, with Jonah representing the Hebrew people. It is interesting to note that no matter which of the interpretations is selected as correct, the meaning of the story remains exactly the same!

After three days the fish deposited Jonah on dry land, and God renewed the call for Jonah to go and preach to Nineveh. This time Johah went, preached to the people, and was somewhat amazed when they repented as a result of his preaching. When the people repented, God forgave them and decided not to carry out the destruction. This turn of events infuriated Jonah, which leads the reader to the basic point of the story—the reason why Jonah had disobeyed God and had not gone to preach to these people in the first place. It was not because Jonah was afraid of them (though this would have been understandable, given their ferocious reputation) or because Jonah feared the great embarrassment of having his message rejected. Jonah had not gone to Nineveh because he had been afraid that he would be successful! "That is why I made haste to flee to Tarshish; for I knew that thou art a gracious God and merciful, slow to anger, and abounding in steadfast love, and repentest of evil" (4:2). Then Jonah went out of the city to see if perchance God might even yet give these sinful people their just desserts. At this point God did some additional "appointing": a plant grew up to shade Jonah's head from the sun. The next day, however,

God appointed a worm to attack the plant, so that it died. And Jonah was again exceedingly angry.

God asked Jonah if he were justifiably angry about the plant since he did not make it or cause it to grow. Jonah responded that he did indeed have just cause to be angry. To that reply God asked Jonah, "And should not I pity Nineveh, that great city, in which there are more than a hundred and twenty thousand persons who do not know their right hand from their left, and also much cattle?" (4:11). With this abrupt but dramatic question the Book of Jonah ends.

The story of Jonah seems, therefore, to have been ideally suited for the postexilic era, when exclusivism had become the order of the day. The questions raised by this book seem to be twofold: (1) Does survival mean that the community must turn its back on God's call to be a "light to the nations"? and (2) Is the motivation behind exclusivism really survival alone—or is it something less honorable, namely, the selfish idea that the community should keep the privileges afforded to itself alone because others do not deserve to have them?

Both the Book of Jonah and the Book of Ruth, while good examples of wisdom-story form, are directly connected to the prevailing religious and social situations of the Jewish community in the postexilic times. Some scholars have argued that these two stories are basically good stories but have no real connection with that setting. Others argue that the stories are so pointedly anti-exclusivistic that it would be overlooking the obvious not to make a connection between the exclusivism of the postexilic Hebrew community and the teachings of these books. In either case the point of each story seems to be clear—God cares for and wishes to embrace and be embraced by people other than the "chosen" ones.

The Book of Esther

Like the book of Ecclesiastes, the Book of Esther had a difficult time finding its place among the authoritative writings of the Old Testament. The primary reason for the reluctance of the rabbis to accept this book lay in the fact that God is never mentioned! There is one place where God may be alluded to (4:14), but that is really doubtful. Another reason was the late date for the composition of the book. Scholars are not in agreement about the date for Esther, but most place its origin between 300 and 150 B.C.

Perhaps the major reason for the final decision to include Esther among the canonical books was the fact that it is the one story that explains the origin of the very popular Jewish festival of Purim. This feast seems to have originated during the postexilic period and was first known as "Mordecai's Day." One of the most popular of all the Jewish feasts, Purim was a time for celebrating the survival of the Jewish people in spite of all the hardships and sufferings they had experienced. On this day gifts were exchanged, the poor were remembered, and joy reigned supreme. Wine could be consumed until the participants could not distinguish any difference between "Blessed be Mordecai!" and "Cursed be Haman!"

The exact origin of the feast of Purim is unknown. It appears to have begun somewhere in Persia, but this is not at all certain. Some scholars argue that Purim originated during the Maccabean era (between 175 and 140 B.C.), since the story presupposes a specific persecution. The only persecution known about was that which occurred under the Seleucid king Antiochus IV in 167 B.C. There may have been some historical incident that lay behind the story as we now have it, but the exact historical setting has probably been lost. The background for the account is so firmly linked to the Persian setting that it is difficult not to assume some historical linkage to that time and place. When one recognizes the *story* nature of the account, however, these considerations become rather secondary.

It is obvious that this literary composition is a wisdom-type story that reflects several concerns of the postexilic Jewish community. In the later postexilic period, many Jews from Judah, because of the harsh economic and political realities existent there, began to move into other parts of the Graeco-Roman world. These groups, coupled with those who had remained in Babylonia (and who had come into contact with the Persian environment) and some who were moved forcibly into other areas, constituted what is popularly called the "Dispersion," the scattering of Jewish people around the Graeco-Roman world. Obviously there had to have been some type of thinking as to how these people, separated from the temple and their homeland, could still continue the religion and traditions of their heritage and yet have constant contact with the Gentile world in which they lived. Frequently the Jewish people, both in Judah and elsewhere, were the recipients of intense hatred and persecution. Questions were certainly raised concerning how the people should respond to the hatred directed towards them, how the attacks against them could be dealt with, and how, if possible, such animosity could be averted or blunted. The Book of Esther appears to deal with some of these questions.

The book seems to have emerged from a combination of several older traditions: one about Esther, one about Mordecai and Haman, one about Vashti, and one about a persecution of the Jewish people from which they somehow escaped. Some scholars have argued for a mythological background for the story, centering in a conflict between two Babylonian deities, Marduk and Ishtar, and their Elamite counterparts, Uman and Mashti. However, this interpretation seems a bit farfetched. The basic reason for this writing seems to have been to provide a specific setting for the feast of Purim and to point out certain other ideas of value to the postexilic Jewish community.

Outline of the Book of Esther
   I. How Esther Became Queen: 1–2
   II. The Plot to Destroy the Jews: 3
   III. Mordecai and Esther Work to Save the People: 4–8
   IV. Reversal of Fortunes and the Beginning of Purim: 9–10

The story of Esther is set within the historical period of the Persian Empire, specfically during the time of King Ahasuerus (Xerxes I, 485–464 B.C.). The first chapters tell how Esther, with the assistance of her cousin, Mordecai, became queen. Upon the advice of Mordecai, Esther did not tell the king that she was a Jew, however. At this point in the story Mordecai discovered a plot against the king's life and sent word to him by way of Esther.

The king then promoted Haman the Agagite to a position of high authority. People were supposed to bow down before anyone holding this high office. Naturally Mordecai would not do this, which infuriated Haman. (It is interesting to note that this story picks up on the ancient enmity between the Benjaminites and the Agagites; see 1 Samuel 15:7.) Upon learning that Mordecai was a Jew, Haman devised a plot to kill all the Jews in Persia! He convinced the king that a group of people in the kingdom was disloyal and obeyed different laws. He urged that the king allow him to eliminate them, and he promised the king the sum of ten thousand talents if he were allowed to carry out this plan. The king agreed and handed over the disposition of the matter to Haman.

The day on which the annihilation was to take place was determined
by the casting of the lot. (The word for "lot" was *Pur*, hence the word
for the feast of *Purim*.) "Letters were sent by couriers to all the king's
provinces, to destroy, to slay, and to annihilate all Jews, young and
old, women and children, in one day . . . and to plunder their goods"
(3:13).

When Mordecai learned of this, he was naturally greatly distressed.
Esther was informed of the problem and, with Mordecai's advice, moved
boldly to attempt to have the king rescind the order. She asked the king
to come to a dinner along with Haman (who thought that all was going
well for him). Haman even had a gallows built especially for Mordecai,
which was fifty cubits high (between 75 and 85 feet!).

In the meantime the king learned that nothing had been done to honor
Mordecai for his part in thwarting the assassination attempt against
him. At that moment Haman entered the king's presence and was asked
what could be done to honor someone special to the king. Thinking
that the recognition was meant for himself, Haman outlined a long list
of honors. When Haman finished the list, the king ordered that Haman
see that all of these things were done for Mordecai!

Haman was then summoned to the feast with the king and Esther.
During this time Esther had told the king that she and her people were
to be annihilated and asked the king to intervene and to spare them.
The king, still not understanding exactly what was happening, asked
who was responsible for this. Whereupon Esther said, "A foe and
enemy! This wicked Haman!" (7:6). When the angry king left for a
few moments, Haman fell on Esther's couch to beg for his life. At that
moment the king reentered the room and mistook the intentions of
Haman. Haman's fate was sealed, needless to say, and he was hanged
on the very gallows he had prepared for Mordecai. The edict against
the Jews was negated by enacting another edict which allowed the Jews
to defend themselves and to kill their enemies on a specific day. In
fact, they were given two days on which to accomplish these ends in
the city, and seventy-five thousand of their enemies were killed.

The story says that the Jews, while being allowed to kill their enemies,
were not allowed to take any plunder. The intent of this item probably
was to emphasize that the people were to defend themselves only, not
to use violence for personal gain. Another major emphasis of this story
is sometimes overlooked by interpreters. This story appears to argue

for a positive attitude toward relationships between Jews and Gentiles. Not all Gentiles were evil and anti-Jewish; relationships with Gentiles could be good both for individual Jewish persons and for the larger Jewish community. In fact it appears that the story suggested that some of the negativism directed against Jews may have been the result of their own attitudes and reactions to situations. There seems to have been a clear call here for good relationships with non-Jews and perhaps encouragement for Jews to become involved in civil governments as a possible way to assist the Jewish people as a whole.

Many modern interpreters are puzzled by what to make of this story. Why should such a vindictive type of teaching be a part of sacred Scripture? As mentioned before, this book almost did not get into the canon. It did so primarily because it formed the basis for the very popular feast of Purim. Beyond that, however, there are some peculiar teachings contained in the book. But if one remembers that this is a wisdom *story,* some of the objections may be avoided.

One finds here the call to the Jewish people to be faithful to the traditions of the community and the resultant triumph if those traditions were kept. There was also the call for positive relationships with Gentiles, even to the point of marrying them and working in their governmental structures and being loyal to them.

Basically, however, the book offered encouragement to the Jewish communities who obviously were suffering periodic persecution by people who hated them for varieties of reasons. The story offered hope in the postexilic period to the Jewish people who were quite poor, vulnerable, and sometimes persecuted. While modern people usually do not condone the slaughter of enemies, the call to defend what one believes in and to weather the "slings and arrows of outrageous fortune" and to keep one's integrity in the face of overwhelming power may be messages that need reinstituting today.

The Song of Songs

The question of whether to include the Song of Songs among the wisdom materials has been debated for some time. Many scholars include this book among the wisdom traditions, however, for they believe that its attribution to Solomon is evidence of that classification. Some interpreters further argue that to investigate human love would have been a part of the task of the wisdom schools.

What the book is about becomes clear rather quickly as one reads the materials. It is a description and an exaltation of the joys of human sexuality! This has caused great embarrassment to those persons who are rather prudish in both the Jewish and Christian traditions. It has been argued by such groups that the book should be understood as an allegory, symbolizing the love of God for God's people. The fact that these poems were sometimes used as songs to be sung in taverns appears to indicate that their symbolic nature was not understood as such initially!

Another approach to these materials has been to interpret them as songs and poetry originally intended to be understood within the context of the marriage covenant. Some have argued that these poems originated from ancient marriage festivals, which frequently lasted for a week or more. It has been postulated that during these times the bride and bridegroom were referred to as the queen and the king. Such an interpretation would sanitize the poems, but whether this theory is correct has been questioned. One of the problems with this approach is that there seem to be three people involved at times, not just two.

In attempting to understand this book and how it may have meaning for today's world, it would be helpful for the modern reader to keep several points in mind. The first is that sexual morality then was quite different from what is accepted today as "normal." Monogamy was not necessarily the order of the day; Solomon had 700 wives and 300 concubines. Furthermore, since the society was male-oriented (and for other reasons also), adultery could not be committed against a wife—only against a husband. There were also periods of time (as in war) when males were scarce, and it became necessary to have multiple wives for the mutual protection of all. Our mores were not necessarily their mores.

Through all of these cultural and historical curiosities, however, one point shone through quite clearly in Hebrew society: human sexuality was to be enjoyed. The act was considered by the Hebrew people as a gift from God, as part of the total enjoyment of life in this world. There was, therefore, no idea that sex as such was inherently evil, as some of the dualistic-thinking Greeks believed (and in whose shadow some people still stand). Such a marvelous gift of God to the human race was meant to be enjoyed! Unfortunately, however, the gift was frequently abused in various ways, necessitating some stringent guidelines to ensure this act against becoming the victim of license and being cheapened to the point of debauchery. Laws were written to regulate sexual activity. This collection of love songs, however, simply exalts the joy and beauty of human sexuality.

There is no agreement among scholars as to how to outline this book. It is uncertain at points as to how many persons are involved in the activities. Some scholars have found only two. Others have argued that there are two males and one female or, conversely, two females and only one male. Some have interpreted the third element as a chorus (similar to the Greek chorus in Greek drama) and therefore find only one man and one woman. Some interpreters find a unity in this material usually resulting from the interpretation that the early chapters are describing courtship and the late chapters the marriage between the lovers. Other commentators argue that there is no real structure or unity in the way the various poetic sections have been woven together.

Whatever the resolution of these questions, the primary question still remains. What is the place of a collection of erotic poems in the sacred canon of Scripture? Perhaps the purpose is to remind human beings of how beautiful the gifts of God are, specifically the gift of sexuality. To debase and cheapen these gifts is to become less than a human being, an animal whose "belly is the stomach" without proper direction in life. The greatest gifts are those most likely to be debased, and the sexual aspects of human life have always been most vulnerable.

The collection of love poems, which is known as the "Greatest Song," exhibits the sheer delight of the gift of human sexual love. It concludes, however, with some teaching that appears to be both direction and warning for persons caught up in the "sexual mores" of life.

> Set me as a seal upon your heart,
>   as a seal upon your arm;
> for love is strong as death. . . .
> Many waters cannot quench love,
>   neither can floods drown it.
> If a man offered for love
>   all the wealth of his house,
>   it would be utterly scorned.
>   —8:6-7

There is a clear direction here for the idea that there is a proper context for sexual relationships. That context is love, and real love cannot be bought. Implicit here is the idea that the practice of sex outside of such a context cheapens this great gift of God and is to be shunned.

Daniel, Chapters 1-6

There is yet another block of material in the Old Testament that falls under the category of wisdom—the first six chapters of the Book of Daniel. These chapters are basically self-contained stories that were told to exalt the Jewish traditions and to encourage the people to keep these traditions in the face of intense pressure, even persecution. The stories were especially applicable for the time in which the Book of Daniel was put into its present form.

The Jewish people in Palestine were undergoing persecution at the hands of the Seleucid king Antiochus IV, who had proscribed Judaism. Antiochus had made it a capital offense to practice the Jewish religion and to keep the regulations of the Torah. Further, Jewish people were being forced to worship Greek gods. The temple was desecrated by the erection of a statue of Zeus within it. Precious items were taken from the temple, and a pig was sacrificed on the altar of Yahweh! Such a situation naturally led to resistance from the Jewish community and harsh repression by the Seleucid authorities.

It was in these times (between 167 and 164 B.C.) that the Book of Daniel was written. The first section of the book (chapters 1–6) was composed of wisdom-type stories told to exalt Jewish traditions and to call for faithfulness despite persecution. The last section of the book (chapters 7–12) consists of apocalyptic visions which belong to a different literary genre and which will not be discussed here.[1] Each of the stories contained in chapters 1–6 is self-contained and reflects the basic problems facing the Jewish people at the time of Antiochus IV. The setting for most of the stories was Babylonia during the time of the Jewish exile (between 587 and 538 B.C.).

The first of the stories was told to demonstrate why it was important to keep the dietary laws. (Antiochus had ordered that these laws be disregarded during the proscription of Judaism in 167 B.C.) The young Jewish boys, Daniel and his three friends, insisted on honoring their

[1] For an introduction to apocalyptic literature see *Daniel and Revelation: A Study of Two Extraordinary Visions,* by James M. Efird (Valley Forge: Judson Press, 1978).

traditions and were rewarded by being wiser and healthier than the others who ate the non-kosher food provided by the king's court. Chapter 3 contains the delightful story of the three Hebrew children and the burning fiery furnace. (The reader is not told where Daniel was during this time!) The king, Nebuchadnezzar, had a huge image of himself made and insisted that all people bow down to it. The Jewish boys refused and were thrown into the furnace, but they were protected by God and emerged from the ordeal unharmed. In these two stories (chapters 1 and 3) the proscription against Judaism during the time of Antiochus was clearly addressed. In the first story the Jewish boys kept the food laws in spite of opposition, and in the second the youths were delivered because they refused to bow down to a golden image (an allusion to the image of Zeus placed in the temple at the time of Antiochus IV).

The story in chapter 4 depicts the great Babylonian king Nebuchadnezzar exalting himself as the greatest person in all the world. Whereupon God struck him with a form of mental disorder that caused him to be properly humbled. Antiochus liked to call himself "Epiphanes," a name which carried the connotation of "God-manifest." The people in 165 B.C. would surely have made the connection between Nebuchadnezzar and Antiochus.

A related incident is reflected in the story in chapter 5. Because the Babylonians had desecrated the sacred vessels from the temple in Jerusalem, the Babylonian kingdom was destroyed. In 169 B.C. Antiochus had plundered the temple in Jerusalem, even stripping gold off the temple facade. It would not have taken a genius to make the connection between the behavior of the Babylonian king and that of Antiochus.

The most famous of all these delightful stories is found in chapter 6, the story of Daniel in the lions' den. In this story, which is similar to that of Esther, certain Persian authorities were jealous of Daniel and tricked the king into signing a proclamation that no one could worship anyone other than the king for a certain period of time. Knowing that Daniel would pray to his God at the appropriate times, they reported him to the king. Though upset over the turn of events, King Darius, was obligated to keep the law. Therefore, Daniel was thrown into the den of lions. The king was so upset that, the story says, ". . . no diversions were brought to him . . ." (6:18), and early the next morning he went to see what had happened to Daniel. Finding that Daniel had been protected from the lions and therefore had passed the "trial by ordeal," the king ordered those who had concocted the plot to be thrown into the lions' den, along with their families. Holding firm in the face of extreme persecution and trusting in God to deliver the people from that persecution were clearly the teachings intended here. Again, the story was directed toward those who were undergoing persecution and facing death for keeping their religious obligations.

The remaining chapter (chapter 2) is a bit more difficult to explain, for it reflects an apocalyptic motif, depicting the flow of history in symbolic images. This chapter should be compared with chapter 7 since they both teach essentially the same idea. There would be four world kingdoms, and after the last one God would smash those powers that have dominated and persecuted God's people. After this the people of God were to have a kingdom of their own with persecution eliminated. The four kingdoms represented in the image were: the Babylonian, the Median, the Persian, and the Greek Empire that was begun by Alexander (the legs of iron) but that was divided into four parts after his death (the feet partly of iron and partly of clay). The story placed the time of the elimination of the persecution during the reign of Alexander's successors, one of whom was Antiochus IV. Again the message is very clear.

One can readily see how the wisdom story came to be one of the primary vehicles for continuing to encourage the Jewish people during the arduous years of the postexilic period and to exalt Jewish ways and traditions in the face of serious opposition from new cultures and unsympathetic people. After reading many of these stories both from within the canon and from among those that did not become canonized, one begins to appreciate how much such stories must have meant to those persons undergoing extremely difficult times. It is also clear how important the diversification and growth of the wisdom traditions were to the continued development of the Jewish faith.

SIX

Coping as a Member of the Kingdom of God

During the period usually designated as the "intertestamental period," the period between the time the last Old Testament book was written (around 165 B.C.) and the appearance of Jesus and the emergence of the early church and its writings, the wisdom movement continued in each of its manifestations. There were those who continued to collect and to propagate practical wisdom, and there were those who continued to write stories to encourage, strengthen, and challenge the Jewish people in particular historical situations.

A very fine example of the continuation of practical wisdom is found in the book known as Ecclesiasticus, or the Wisdom of Ben Sirach. This work is found among the books of the Apocrypha, and it contains a form of wisdom quite similar to the older proverbial type but with significant developments in literary style and in theological matters. The nature of the teachings of Ben Sirach appears to be mainly exhortative, though many other nuances are included as well. This thinker urges people to be involved in life and to participate in it to the fullest, although cautiously at some points. One of the comments he makes is appropriate: "While you are still alive and have breath in you, do not

83

let any one take your place'' (Sirach 33:20, RSV *Common Bible*).

Many other writings emerged from the wisdom schools and traditions during this period. There were additions to Esther (an attempt to make that story more religious), additions to Daniel, the Wisdom of Solomon, the books of Judith and Tobit, and numerous others. All of these writings indicate that the wisdom tradition, methodologies, and ideas were quite prominent in the culture and thought of the times when Jesus appeared in Palestine.

The Wisdom Method and the Teaching of Jesus

When we examine the life and teachings of Jesus as they are preserved in the Synoptic Gospels (Matthew, Mark, and Luke), it is not at all surprising to discover that Jesus taught basically by wisdom methodology. He called an intimate group to be around him so that he could teach them, much like the leader of a wisdom school. His teachings, as one can readily learn by examination of the texts, consist of short pithy sayings, parables, a few allegories, and many figures of speech usually characterized by the element of hyperbole. If the one who is attempting to learn what Jesus intended to teach will keep in mind this wisdom background, that person is not likely to misunderstand, misinterpret, and distort the meaning of these marvelous sayings.

Jesus' Parables: How Their Teachings Are Missed

Most persons are familiar with the parables of Jesus. These are stories drawn from everyday life and told to illustrate a basic point. They usually contain an implicit challenge for the hearers to understand the teaching and to apply it to their daily lives. As already indicated, parables are different from allegories in that a parable makes one basic point (there may be a subpoint or two, however) while an allegory is intended to present the hearer with a story in which each element has some hidden or symbolic meaning. There are a few allegories in the teachings of Jesus (see Matthew 13:24-30, 36-43; 13:47-50), but interestingly enough each of them is already explained, so that there is no reason for us to suggest wild interpretations for them as some have done. The major issue for the student of the teachings of Jesus is to interpret the parable *as a parable,* a story told to illustrate a specific point and to challenge the hearer/reader to act in accordance with the teaching. A rather extensive misuse of the parables lies in the fact that all too often they have been interpreted as if they were allegories. Hidden meanings are found in each detail of the story, which would be acceptable *if* the story were an allegory. Parables are not allegories, however, and should not be interpreted as such.

One of the most common mistakes that preachers make (setting a bad example for lay persons) lies precisely in this area. A parable is read from a Scripture text, and the preacher proceeds to make an allegory of it. The parable of the good Samaritan (Luke 10:29-37) has been expecially vulnerable in this regard. Usually the allegorical (and incorrect) interpretation goes something like this: The road along which the man travels is the road of life, and the man represents every person who, at some point along life's way, experiences evil at the hands of enemies (also given an identity). The process of identifying the priest and the Levite depends upon who is telling the story, but quite frequently it evolves into the priest symbolizing the Roman Catholic church and the Levite the Jewish community. The good Samaritan then can either be "us" or Jesus. The oil poured on the beaten man's wounds has a meaning also, sometimes being understood as the Spirit with its healing power; and the beast upon which the battered man rides is the Word of God, which bears us up in times of trial. The inn naturally refers to "our" church. The innkeeper may then be Jesus (if Jesus is not the good Samaritan) or the church official(s). The two denarii represent the sacraments, Baptism and the Lord's Supper, and the benefactor's comment (that he is going away and will return) could be a reference to Jesus' Second Coming (if the Samaritan is Jesus). It surely goes without saying that this is not the proper way to interpret a parable! In fact, it does real violence to the true meaning of the story.

According to Luke's setting, the parable of the good Samaritan was told in response to a question put to Jesus by one of the Jewish officials: "Who is my neighbor?" After the story, Jesus asked the lawyer who was neighbor to the man in need. The answer was, "The one who showed mercy. . . ." The point of the story as Luke presented it seems to be that every person in need is our neighbor, a simple message but one that has yet to be heard.

Another problem that arises frequently with regard to the interpretation of the parables is that some persons attempt to take small portions of the parables and create theological dogmas from them. One such situation can be illustrated from the famous Lukan parable of the rich man and Lazarus (16:19-31). It is the story of a poor man named Lazarus who begged crumbs from the table of a rich man. When the two men died, Lazarus went to the "bosom of Abraham" and the rich man to the place of torment. In those days there were numerous ideas concerning life after death. This story uses one of those ideas as a supporting device to help illustrate a setting for the main point of the parable. The point is that people who want to be religious will be religious and those who do not will not become believers even if stupendous miracles occur. In other words, real religious faith cannot be based on external signs no matter how marvelous they are. One can see that the concept of life after death used in this story was the one appropriate for the point to be made in this particular story. Some persons, however, have taken the part of this narrative dealing with the afterlife (vv. 22-26) and have made it into an absolutely literal and theological dogma of what happens after death to believers and/or non-believers. That is an illegitimate use of this text.

There are some Christians who hold to the view of "universal salvation," the view that *all* persons will somehow be ultimately "saved." To support their ideas these persons naturally want to make use of Scripture, since that is considered authoritative evidence and support for theological doctrines. Whether or not universal salvation is a legitimate doctrine is not the issue here. The point is that some persons use a short clause in one of Jesus' parables as support for that theory. In the parable of the lost sheep in Luke 15:1-7, there is the clause ". . . until he [the owner] finds it." The "theology" of this clause is understood to be that God will ultimately save all of the lost. Such a use of this passage is fanciful, a case of reading into a casual comment in a story meanings that obviously were not originally intended. The point of the parable is the value of the lost sheep and the effort the owner makes to find it—nothing more, nothing less.

In the very short parable of the treasure hidden in a field (Matthew 13:44) Jesus describes a situation that often occurs in life. A person finds something of value and does everything possible to obtain it. This is the point of the parable—that participation in the kingdom of God is worth every effort a person can make and everything a person has. Some persons, however, become concerned over the problem of the ethics involved within this story. Is Jesus condoning the practice of discovering something valuable, concealing its existence, and then cheating the owner out of it? Does this mean that in personal or business life Jesus has sanctioned this type of behavior? If this teaching were direct and straightforward, these questions could be relevant, but in a parable such details are not part of the point of the story. They are only part of the general scene or setting for the story, which sets the stage for the main point. To make theological or ethical doctrines, therefore, from general settings in a parable is to misunderstand the nature of the wisdom teaching. Careful and common-sense study of these stories will guard against fanciful interpretations never intended by the storytellers.

Jesus' Wisdom Sayings: When Literalism Is Dangerous

If indeed the parables of Jesus are sometimes grievously misunderstood, some of his wisdom sayings are even more vulnerable to misinterpretation. In some instances the teachings are ripped from their larger contexts and literalized into absolute legalisms. They are not recognized as wisdom sayings and/or hyperbole. For example, in Matthew 5:29-30 one reads, "If your right eye causes you to sin, pluck it out and throw it away. . . . And if your right hand causes you to sin, cut it off and throw it away; it is better that you lose one of your members than that your whole body go into [Gehenna (a place for outcasts, the unclean, and so forth)]." It should be obvious that this teaching was never meant to be interpreted literally. The basic point is to illustrate the extreme seriousness of choosing to accept God's gift of kingdom life. What is being offered by God is of ultimate importance and significance, and the rejection of this gift carries with it serious consequences.

Another illustration comes from the same setting (Matthew's account of the Sermon on the Mount) when Jesus was teaching how to break the cycle of revenge, which is a never-ending sequence of cause and effect. The advice he gave was that one should deal with this cycle by not always insisting on one's right of response. It is here that one reads the well-known words, "But if any one strikes you on the right cheek, turn to him the other also . . ." (5:39). Some persons have made of this passage an absolute teaching by Jesus that his followers all be pacifists. One may wish to be a pacifist, but such a position cannot be supported merely by a literal interpretation of this verse. If such an interpretation were true, what would one then do with other passages in which Jesus told the disciples, "And let him who has no sword sell his mantle and buy one" (Luke 22:36)? Or "Do not think that I have come to bring peace on earth; I have not come to bring peace, but a sword" (Matthew 10:34)? How does one make sense of such passages that appear to be directly opposite in meaning? The answer lies in the fact that the interpreter needs to learn how to interpret these wisdom sayings as *wisdom sayings*. Absolutizing them into legalistic commandments apart from their context causes the interpreter to miss the point of the sayings entirely.

There have been numerous attempts to understand the sayings of Jesus that were collected by Matthew to form the Sermon on the Mount (chapters 5–7). By failing to recognize these teachings as wisdom types, many readers have been greatly distressed since no one can literally keep all the commands that Jesus gave in this passage. One ingenious attempt to solve the problem was to understand the teachings as authoritative for only a short period of time. The argument was that Jesus did not expect his followers to be able to keep these commands for a long time; tenacity was unnecessary anyway since Jesus believed that the end was to come in the very near future. These commands were then interpreted as an interim ethic, binding on the disciples for only a short while until the consummation of the kingdom came.

Two comments should be made about this approach. The first is that if the interpreter recognizes the teachings as wisdom sayings, which should be understood for the meaning inherent in each saying rather than an absolute ethical legalism set in stone for all ages, the points become rather clear and obvious. The setting for each saying frequently assists the interpreter in being able to understand the meanings of the teaching. The second comment may well be put best by raising a question: Why is it that persons attempt to make of Jesus' teachings absolute legalisms when Jesus came to do away with precisely just such an interpretation of the law? This does not mean that everything is relative, but it does caution the interpreter of Jesus' teachings to be aware of substituting one set of legalisms for another.

The Purpose of Wisdom Sayings of Jesus

Most of Jesus' teachings in the Synoptic Gospels revolve around the nature of the kingdom of God, how one enters that kingdom, and what is expected of a member of that group. These teachings are basically done in wisdom form—parables, a few allegories, short pithy sayings, and sayings characterized by hyperbole. Space does not permit the explication of each of these marvelous sayings, but it is hoped that these guidelines will assist the interpreter to understand better the teachings of Jesus. It appears that these sayings were intended to equip the members of God's kingdom to cope with life in accord with the demands of the kingdom and to assist members to cope with the world and the people of the world who do not accept the values and life-style of kingdom members.

Epilogue

Our purpose in this short work has been to examine the phenomenon known as the wisdom movement, as it is exemplified in the biblical materials. We have learned that this tradition had a long history and included different ideas and literary devices. That this type of thinking was popular is evidenced in the fact that there were many other books of the wisdom type current in ancient times which did not find a place in the canon of inspired works.

Perhaps the reason for the immense popularity of these writings was that the wisdom tradition dealt with life as it really was and offered suggestions as to how best to get along in this world. Every person is eager to learn how to cope with the problems of life; every person longs to have as much happiness in this world as possible; every person wants to know "why?" when things do not go according to plan; every person wants to find meaning and purpose in life. Wisdom literature and thought spoke to these very issues. It is not surprising, therefore, that such ideas were popular with people even before the first written documents.

The persons who formed the ranks of the "wise" in Israel understood that true wisdom had to have a religious base. Life can have no real meaning or purpose or direction by itself. It is only because of God that life's struggles are worth the effort. It is only because of God that life has a sense of direction and purpose. Even the skepticism and realism of Qoheleth could not obliterate the personality of God, who could somehow make life mean something if a person were willing to struggle with whatever came. It is no wonder, then, that these teachings and books were exceedingly popular! Neither is it surprising that when Jesus came, much of his popularity with the people lay in the fact that he taught them in the wisdom tradition. He instructed them that life did have meaning, and he offered directions about how best to live, not simply as citizens of this world but as citizens of the kingdom of God.

The truly wise never taught that life was easy; it was always depicted as a struggle. For whatever reason, that struggle may seem easier to some than to others. External circumstances may make life rosy for one person and difficult for another. Sometimes life is normal; sometimes it is anything but that! Through it all, however, there is the sincere conviction—from authors of Proverbs to Job to Qoheleth to Jesus—that God *can* make sense of life. And if our lives are dedicated to God's service, they will have meaning and direction and purpose. If this were not true, there would be no real meaning to life and its struggles.

Suggestions for Further Study

General Books on Wisdom

Brueggemann, Walter, *In Man We Trust: The Neglected Side of Biblical Faith*. Atlanta: John Knox Press, 1972.

Crenshaw, James L., *Old Testament Wisdom: An Introduction*. Atlanta: John Knox Press, 1981.

Murphy, Roland E., *Wisdom Literature: Ruth, Esther, Job, Proverbs, Ecclesiastes, Canticles*. The Forms of the Old Testament Literature Series, vol. 13. Grand Rapids: Wm. B. Eerdmans Publishing Co., 1981.

Scott, R. B. Y., *The Way of Wisdom*. New York: Macmillan Inc., 1971.

Von Rad, Gerhard, *Wisdom in Israel*. Trans. James D. Martin. Nashville:˙Abingdon Press, 1973.

Wood, James, *Wisdom Literature: An Introduction*. London: Gerald Duckworth & Co., Ltd., 1967.

Works on Specific Books

Fuerst, Wesley J., *The Books of Ruth, Esther, Ecclesiastes, the Song of Songs, Lamentations*. Cambridge Bible Commentaries on the New English Bible, Old Testament Series. New York: Cambridge University Press, 1975.

Gordis, Robert, *The Book of Job: Commentary, New Translation and Special Studies*. New York: The Jewish Theological Seminary of America, 1977.

————— , *The Book of God and Man*. Chicago: University of Chicago Press, 1978.

————— , *Koheleth: The Man and His World: A Study of Ecclesiastes*. Rev. ed. New York: Schocken Books, Inc., 1967.

Habel, Norman C., *The Book of Job*. Cambridge Bible Commentaries on the New English Bible, Old Testament Series. New York: Cambridge University Press, 1975.

————— , *Job*. Atlanta: John Knox Press, 1981.

Hammer, Raymond, *The Book of Daniel*. Cambridge Bible Commentaries on the New English Bible, Old Testament Series. New York: Cambridge University Press, 1976.

Hartman, Louis F., and DiLella, A. A., *The Book of Daniel: A New Translation with Introduction and Commentary*. Anchor Bible Series. Garden City, N.Y.: Doubleday & Co., Inc., 1978.

Lacocque, André, *The Book of Daniel*. Trans. David Pellaver. Atlanta: John Knox Press, 1978.

McKane, William, *Proverbs: A New Approach*. Old Testament Library Series. Philadelphia: Westminster Press, 1970.

Moore, Carey A., *Esther*. Anchor Bible Series. Garden City, N. Y.: Doubleday & Co., Inc., 1971.

Murphy, Roland E., *The Psalms, Job*. Proclamation Commentaries: The Old Testament Witness for Preaching. Philadelphia: Fortress Press, 1977.

————— , *Seven Books of Wisdom*. Milwaukee: Bruce Publishing Co., 1960.

Pope, Marvin H., ed., *Job*. Rev. ed. Garden City, N.Y.: Doubleday & Co., Inc., 1973. (Not for beginners!)

Porteous, Norman, *Daniel: A Commentary*. Philadelphia: Westminster Press, 1965.

Rowley, H. H., *Job*. Rev. ed. New Century Bible Commentary Series.

Grand Rapids: Wm. B. Eerdmans Publishing Co., 1976.

Scott, R. B. Y., *Proverbs and Ecclesiastes*. Anchor Bible Series: Garden City, N. Y.: Doubleday & Co., Inc., 1965.

Terrien, Samuel, *The Book of Job: Introduction and Exegesis*. The Interpreter's Bible, edited by G. A. Buttrick *et al.*, vol. 3. New York: Abingdon Press, 1954.

_____ , *Job: Poet of Existence*. Indianapolis: The Bobbs-Merrill Co., Inc., 1957.

Whybray, R. N., *The Book of Proverbs*. Cambridge Bible Commentaries on the New English Bible, Old Testament Series. New York: Cambridge University Press, 1972.

Made in the USA
Columbia, SC
04 May 2017